RAINBOW

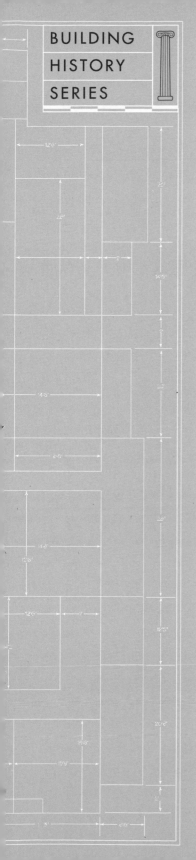

THE
MEDIEVAL
CASTLE

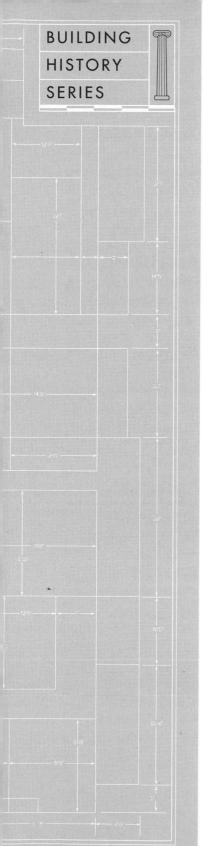

BUILDING
HISTORY
SERIES

THE
MEDIEVAL
CASTLE

by Don Nardo

Lucent Books, Inc., San Diego, California

Library of Congress Cataloging-in-Publication Data

Nardo, Don, 1947–
    The medieval castle / by Don Nardo.
      p.   cm. — (Building history series)
    Includes bibliographical references and index.
    Summary: Describes how medieval castles were built and
examines the daily lives of those inhabiting them.
    ISBN 1-56006-430-7 (alk. paper)
    1. Castles—Juvenile literature.   2. Civilization, Medieval—
Juvenile literature.   [1. Castles. 2. Civilization, Medieval.]
    I. Title. II. Series.
    GT3550.N37   1998
    940.1—dc21   97-34638
                                                  CIP
                                                  AC

CONTENTS

FOREWORD

Throughout history, as civilizations have evolved and prospered, each has produced unique buildings and architectural styles. Combining the need for both utility and artistic expression, a society's buildings, particularly its large-scale public structures, often reflect the individual character traits that distinguish it from other societies. In a very real sense, then, buildings express a society's values and unique characteristics in tangible form. As scholar Anita Abramovitz comments in her book *People and Spaces*, "Our ways of living and thinking—our habits, needs, fear of enemies, aspirations, materialistic concerns, and religious beliefs—have influenced the kinds of spaces that we build and that later surround and include us."

That specific types and styles of structures constitute an outward expression of the spirit of an individual people or era can be seen in the diverse ways that various societies have built palaces, fortresses, tombs, churches, government buildings, sports arenas, public works, and other such monuments. The ancient Greeks, for instance, were a supremely rational people who originated Western philosophy and science, including the atomic theory and the realization that the earth is a sphere. Their public buildings, epitomized by Athens's magnificent Parthenon temple, were equally rational, emphasizing order, harmony, reason, and above all, restraint.

By contrast, the Romans, who conquered and absorbed the Greek lands, were a highly practical people preoccupied with acquiring and wielding power over others. The Romans greatly admired and readily copied elements of Greek architecture, but modified and adapted them to their own needs. "Roman genius was called into action by the enormous practical needs of a world empire," wrote historian Edith Hamilton. "Rome met them magnificently. Buildings tremendous, indomitable, amphitheaters where eighty thousand could watch a spectacle, baths where three thousand could bathe at the same time."

In medieval Europe, God heavily influenced and motivated the people, and religion permeated all aspects of society, molding people's worldviews and guiding their everyday actions. That spiritual mindset is reflected in the most important medieval structure—the Gothic cathedral—which, in a sense, was a model of heavenly cities. As scholar Anne Fremantle so elegantly phrases it, the cathedrals were "harmonious elevations of stone and glass reaching up to heaven to seek and receive the light [of God]."

Our more secular modern age, in contrast, is driven by the realities of a global economy, advanced technology, and mass communications. Responding to the needs of international trade and the growth of cities housing millions of people, today's builders construct engineering marvels, among them towering skyscrapers of steel and glass, mammoth marine canals, and huge and elaborate rapid transit systems, all of which would have left their ancestors, even the Romans, awestruck.

In examining some of humanity's greatest edifices, Lucent Books' Building History series recognizes this close relationship between a society's historical character and its buildings. Each volume in the series begins with a historical sketch of the people who erected the edifice, exploring their major achievements as well as the beliefs, customs, and societal needs that dictated the variety, functions, and styles of their buildings. A detailed explanation of how the selected structure was conceived, designed, and built, to the extent that this information is known, makes up the majority of the volume.

Each volume in the Lucent Building History series also includes several special features that are useful tools for additional research. A chronology of important dates gives students an overview, at a glance, of the evolution and use of the structure described. Sidebars create a broader context by adding further details on some of the architects, engineers, and construction tools, materials, and methods that made each structure a reality, as well as the social, political, and/or religious leaders and movements that inspired its creation. Useful maps help the reader locate the nations, cities, streets, and individual structures mentioned in the text; and numerous diagrams and pictures illustrate tools and devices that bring to life various stages of construction. Finally, each volume contains two bibliographies, one for student research, the other listing works the author consulted in compiling the book.

Taken as a whole, these volumes, covering diverse ancient and modern structures, constitute not only a valuable research tool, but also a tribute to the human spirit, a fascinating exploration of the dreams, skills, ingenuity, and dogged determination of the great peoples who shaped history.

IMPORTANT DATES IN THE BUILDING OF MEDIEVAL CASTLES

1096
Pope Urban II launches the first of several Crusades, during which European soldiers and engineers will be influenced by Eastern castle-building techniques.

ca. 1250
Early Greek warriors besiege the independent trading city of Troy, in northwestern Asia Minor.

B.C. ca. 6500
Impressive castlelike defenses are built at sites in Asia Minor (Turkey) and other parts of the Near East.

1080
The Normans erect a powerful castle at Launceston, in southwestern England.

1137
After a three-month-long siege, Exeter Castle, north of London, falls when its well dries up.

ca. 30
Herod the Great builds the fort at Masada, which has many features resembling those of later medieval castles.

| B.C. ca. 6500 | ca. 1280 | ca. 1250 | 213–212 | ca. 30 | A.D. 1066 | 1080 | 1096 | ca. 1110 | 1137 |

ca. 1280
The ancient Egyptians besiege Hittite castles in the Near East.

ca. 1110
A group of crusaders takes over and rebuilds a Muslim castle in Syria, thereafter known as the Krak of the Knights, the mightiest of all crusader fortresses.

213–212
The Romans besiege Syracuse, where they encounter formidable defensive schemes and devices engineered by Archimedes.

Sirmione Castle, Italy

A.D. 1066
The Norman lord William, later known as "the Conqueror," crosses the English Channel and subdues the Anglo-Saxons at the Battle of Hastings; in the succeeding decades the Normans build many motte-and-bailey and shell-keep castles across the English countryside, helping to consolidate their conquest.

1168–1189
The English king Henry II builds Dover Castle, guarding the English Channel.

1224
England's King Henry III takes Bedford Castle after an eight-week siege.

1453
Constantinople falls to the Ottoman Turks after a fifty-three-day siege marked by a devastating barrage of cannon fire.

1562
The English government orders that Tickhill and other castles, now obsolete as fortresses, be maintained as "ancient monuments."

1215
England's King John signs the Magna Carta, conceding certain rights and powers to his leading subjects.

Arundel Castle, England

| 1168–1189 | 1204 | 1215 | 1216 | 1224 | 1271 | 1272–1307 | 1388 | ca. 1446–1453 | 1453 | 1494 | 1562 |

1216
Dover Castle withstands a siege led by France's Louis the Dauphin.

ca. 1446–1453
Using cannons, the French subdue the English castles of northern France with astonishing speed.

1272–1307
Reign of England's Edward I, one of the most prodigious castle builders ever.

1271
The Krak of the Knights falls to the Muslim sultan Beibars I.

1494
Utilizing new, more advanced cannons, France's Charles VIII invades Italy, capturing some castles in as little as eight hours.

1204
After French soldiers gain entry through a latrine drain, France's king Philip II takes Château-Gaillard, Richard I's castle stronghold in northern France.

INTRODUCTION

It would undoubtedly be difficult to find any modern resident of Europe or North America older than the age of two or three who does not recognize the image of the medieval stone castle. Indeed, thanks to a seemingly endless stream of children's stories, novels, comic books, magazines, TV programs, and movies, nearly everyone is familiar with medieval castle dwellers such as King Arthur; and the image of a castle's towering walls and battlements immediately evokes visions of knights in armor, fierce sieges, and powerful lords dominating poor, beleaguered peasants.

Such instant identification of, and often with, castles and the medieval lore surrounding them is no accident. The traditions, social customs, literary styles, politics, and military institutions and strategies making up that lore constitute an integral part of the formative development of Western civilization. In fact, the modern world was in large degree shaped by the European world of medieval times, also known as the Middle Ages. And castles dominated the life of the High Middle Ages, the period lasting from about A.D. 1000 to 1400. This was an age when petty kings and powerful local lords ruled the many hundreds of small kingdoms and large landed estates, or manors, that dotted Europe. Each domain, including its hundreds or thousands of peasant farmers and villagers, was overseen and controlled by a lord residing in one or more stone castles. At the same time, complex and constantly shifting alliances and hostilities among competing lords led to periodic attacks and counterattacks on and from castle strongholds. Noted medieval scholars Joseph and Frances Gies comment:

A multitude of spires grace this castle illustration from the fifteenth-century Book of Hours.

> Enemy castles were major political-military objectives in themselves, and many were sited specifically to bar invasion routes. Typically the castle stood on high ground

commanding a river crossing, a river confluence, a stretch of navigation, a coastal harbor, a mountain pass, or some other strategically important feature. The castle inside a city could be defended long after the city had been taken, and an unsubdued castle garrison could sally out and reoccupy the town the moment the enemy left. Even a rural castle could not safely be bypassed, because its garrison could cut the invader's supply lines. The mobility of the garrison—nearly always supplied with horses—conferred a large strategic radius for many purposes: raiding across a border, furnishing a supply base for an army on the offensive, interrupting road or river traffic at a distance. For all these reasons, medieval military science was the science of the attack and defense of castles.

Thus, in the hands of an elite and powerful few, castles became both instruments of political and social control and strategic tools for offense and defense. In short, as historian Robin Fedden puts it, "castles were the key to the land. If the invader wished to conquer territory permanently, the castles had first to be reduced." Because of this central position that castles occupied in medieval society, examining their development, construction, and military use reveals much about the needs and attitudes of their builders and thereby briefly opens a window onto a unique and fascinating bygone era that has consistently captured the imaginations of later ages.

An Inspiration for Medieval Builders: Forts and Sieges in Ancient Times

Even if one had never seen or heard of medieval castles, it would be easy to deduce that they must be very old; for the roots of the words *medieval* and *castle* predate English and other modern languages. The term *medieval* evolved from the Latin phrase *medium aevum*, meaning "the age in the middle," which also gave rise to the synonym for medieval times—the Middle Ages. And the modern word *castle* comes from the Latin *castellum*, a diminutive form of *castrum*, meaning a "fortified place." By the thirteenth or fourteenth century, *castellum* had changed to *castel* in Old French, and a simple repositioning of the last two letters produced the familiar English version.

Stone Castles—a Very Ancient Idea

Yet the origins of medieval castles are actually far older than the words describing them. The use of stone to fortify towns, palaces, and military stations is a very ancient idea. As early as 6500 B.C., for example, the town at Çatal Hüyük in what is now central Turkey featured impressive castlelike defenses, as noted archaeologist Trevor Watkins describes:

> The square, flat-roofed houses were built side by side like a pile of children's building blocks, pushed together. Access to each house was by means of a door at roof-level, from which a steep ladder led down into the living area. Circulation [movement] around the settlement was across the flat roofs. The edge of such a settlement would have presented a solid, blank wall to any intruder

or attacker. Once the ladders . . . were drawn up, the set-
tlement would have been impregnable.

Other similar fortified sites apparently existed in the Near East
before that at Çatal Hüyük, although no one knows when the
first such structures were built.

Later Near Eastern cultures, including the Babylonians and
Assyrians (both inhabiting the Tigris–Euphrates River valley),
and the Hittites (in central and eastern Turkey), certainly utilized early versions of castles. These structures had many features almost identical to those of medieval times, including
stone curtain walls (outer defenses) and keeps (inner towers or

BABYLON'S FABLED WALLS

The famous Greek historian Herodotus, now often referred to as the "Father of History," visited the Near East
in the fifth century B.C. and saw firsthand the magnificent
fortifications surrounding the ancient city of Babylon. This
excerpt from his *Histories* describes the city's imposing
walls, its moat, and two inner fortresses, or keeps, all of
which were large-scale ancient versions
of identical features found in most medieval European castles.

[Babylon] is surrounded by a broad
deep moat full of water, and within the
moat there is a wall fifty cubits [about
seventy-five feet] wide and two hundred [three hundred feet] high. . . . On
the top of the wall they constructed,
along each edge, a row of one-roomed
buildings facing inwards with enough
space between for a four-horse chariot
to pass. There are a hundred gates in
the circuit of the wall, all of bronze. . . . The great
wall I have described is the chief armor of the city;
but there is a second one within it, hardly less strong
though smaller. There is a fortress in the middle of
each half of the city: in one [rests] the royal palace,
surrounded by a wall of great strength, in the other
the temple of Bel [an important Babylonian god].

*A reconstruction of the city of
Babylon at the height of its power and prosperity.*

forts); battlements with alternating merlons (square notches) and crenels (openings); and hoardings (or hoards; temporary wooden platforms built out from the tops of the walls). These early castles also underwent sieges not unlike those of the Middle Ages. For example, a surviving Egyptian wall drawing, dating from about 1280 B.C., shows a Hittite fortress being besieged by Egyptian troops. The fortress, writes Sidney Toy, a noted expert on ancient fortifications,

> is surrounded by two lines of curtain walls, and has a rectangular keep . . . within the second wall. There is a large gateway in the outer wall, flanked by a tower on either side. Turrets rise from the inner wall, and all the walls and towers are surmounted [topped] by embattled parapets. The city is being stormed by the Egyptians, and the Hittites are fighting from the battlements of all three lines of fortification. Hoards . . . are projected out from the parapets of the inner wall and . . . keep, and men are fighting from them. The weapons used are bows and arrows and lances. The Egyptians advance under the cover of long shields . . . and the attack is by means of scaling ladders.

OTHER ANCIENT NEAR EASTERN FORTRESSES

Not long after the siege depicted in this wall drawing, a much more famous siege took place near Turkey's northwestern coast. Perhaps about 1250 B.C., a powerful Greek army sailed across the Aegean Sea, the narrow Mediterranean inlet separating Greece and Turkey, and attacked the fortress city of Troy. This siege became the basis for a series of exciting tales about the Trojan War, especially the one told in Greece's great national epic, the *Iliad*, traditionally credited to a ninth- or eighth-century B.C. blind poet named Homer. Troy's massive castlelike walls were excavated beginning in the 1870s, and they revealed a number of defensive features strikingly similar to those of large-scale medieval fortifications.

A particularly prominent example can be seen in Troy's eastern defenses. The eastern gate was protected by two high stone towers, which stood on either side of it. Part of the main town wall ran away at a right angle from the inner tower until it reached a much larger tower, the so-called east tower, which ex-

This fanciful scene, painted ca. 1464, depicts the famous Trojan horse entering Troy. Note the Greek warriors hiding inside the wooden horse.

tended outward from the wall. Meanwhile, another wall, parallel to the town wall, extended from the outer edge of the outer gate tower. The sort of enclosed space created by these walls and towers was called a "barbican" in medieval times. To reach

Troy's eastern gate, an attacking enemy force had to enter the barbican, passing by the massive east tower, from which the defenders fired a deadly barrage of arrows, rocks, and other missiles; then the attackers had to continue through the enclosure, where more missiles rained down from the town wall; and finally they had to face the barrier of the gate towers, which were also heavily defended. It is not difficult to see why the Greeks, in Homer's tale, were unable to breach the citadel's gates and had to resort to the trickery of the "Trojan horse." (Greek soldiers hid inside the immense wooden horse; after the Trojans pulled this "gift" into the city, the Greeks climbed out and opened the gates from the inside.) Medieval builders incorporated barbicans very much like that guarding Troy's eastern defenses into the castles at Caerphilly and Conway, both built in Wales in the late 1200s A.D.

Another ancient Near Eastern fortress, Masada, near the western edge of the Dead Sea in Palestine, is particularly striking for its resemblance to a medieval castle. Built about 30 B.C. by the local ruler Herod the Great, the fortress stands on a plateau at the top of a steep hill. The plateau was originally surrounded by a stone curtain wall 18 feet high and 12 feet thick, which enclosed a large open courtyard, or bailey, and featured

Visible here are some of the ruins of the hill fortress of Masada, in Palestine, which originally displayed many castlelike features.

thirty-eight stone guard towers, each 75 feet high. Inside the western end of the enclosure rose a rectangular fortified palace, the keep, itself surrounded by high walls and guarded by four 90-foot-high towers. In overall design, the medieval fortresses at Arques and Falaise in France and at Rochester and Scarborough in England closely resemble that at Masada, which predated them by more than a thousand years. Rochester Castle, built about 1130 some twenty-five miles east of London, features a massive keep with four corner towers similar to those that originally graced Masada's keep. The walls of Rochester's keep are 12 feet thick and 113 feet high, and the towers rise another 12 feet above the walls.

LETHAL ADVANCES IN SIEGE CRAFT

Such similarities between the fortresses and sieges of the ancient Near East and those of the Middle Ages are hardly a matter of coincidence. Near Eastern examples strongly influenced those of the ancient Greeks, which inspired those of the Romans and other later ancient peoples, which, in their turn, influenced medieval castles and siege craft. Indeed, many of sieges that took place in the ancient Greek and Roman world differed from their medieval counterparts primarily in the costumes worn and languages spoken by their participants.

Great advances were made in both stone fortifications and siege craft in the fourth and third centuries B.C. by the Greeks, motivated partly by their introduction of the catapult and other missile-throwing siege engines. These developments reached their height during the terrible wars fought in the four decades following Alexander the Great's death (323 B.C.) by his generals (the Diadochi, or "Successors") and their sons (the Epigoni, or "Descendants"). The offensive siege weapons used by the Diadochi and Epigoni included not only catapults and other relatively new inventions, but also unusually large and destructive versions of devices known from earlier times. Perhaps the most dramatic example was the siege tower, a multistoried wooden contraption that moved on wheels. Attacking soldiers hid inside and fired arrows as the tower approached a defensive wall; upon reaching the wall, they dropped a ramp onto the top of the battlement and swarmed out to engage the defenders in hand-to-hand combat. Siege towers also provided cover for attackers wielding battering rams or shovels for digging under the walls.

The biggest and most lethal siege tower known in ancient times was built by the Athenian engineer Epimachus for the Greek prince and general Demetrius, whose prowess in attacking cities earned him the nickname of Poliorcetes, or "the Besieger." The tower had at least nine stories, reaching a total height of nearly 140 feet, a base 72 feet square, and weighed an estimated 150 tons. Most of the lower stories contained catapults and spear-throwing machines, which fired through rectangular openings; when these devices were inactive, the openings were protected by wooden doors that men inside raised and lowered using chains. The tower's outside surface was covered with metal plates to reduce the risk of fire damage. It rested on eight wheels, each 15 feet in diameter, which turned by means of a capstan, a vertical rotating shaft with handles projecting outward like the spokes of a bicycle wheel. Because of the tower's tremendous weight, the capstan, resting on the floor of the lowest level, directly above the wheels, required at least two hundred men to turn it. Few, if any, medieval siege towers were as large, complex, and well protected as Poliorcetes' monstrous version (partly because medieval rulers lacked the enormous wealth, resources, and manpower that he had at his disposal).

As a siege tower makes contact with a castle wall, attackers rush across a gangway to fight hand to hand with the defenders.

DEFENSIVE DEVICES

To counter such formidable offensive machines, Greek engineers marshaled an array of effective defensive schemes and devices, mostly improved or more elaborate adaptations of those used by earlier peoples. The moat, which would later become a characteristic feature of medieval castles, was an important example. According to military historian John Warry:

> As a defense against the approach of siege towers, deep moats were often dug in front of the walls of a fortified position. Such moats had been dug in front of the

Athenian city walls after the battle of Chaeronea [in 338 B.C., where Macedonia's King Philip II defeated the Athenians, who feared he might next march on Athens] and they were improved during the course of the succeeding century. On archaeological evidence, these moats appear to have reached a depth of 13 feet and a width of 33 feet. In some instances, moats were filled with water; when they surrounded cities, further protection was often given by a wall or palisade [stockade] on the inner edge.

Another defensive feature the Greeks exploited to great advantage was the loophole, commonly called an arrow loop in medieval times, a small opening in a wall through which defenders shot missile weapons. The most celebrated use of loopholes in this period was during the Roman siege of the Sicilian Greek city of Syracuse in 213–212 B.C. When the Roman commander, Marcellus, brought his ships near the city's seaward side, he encountered a surprise prepared by Syracuse's resident genius, Archimedes, the greatest inventor of ancient times. According to the second-century B.C. Greek historian Polybius:

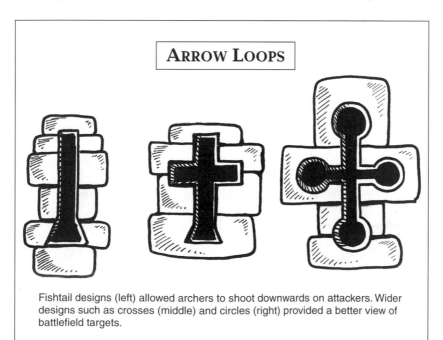

ARROW LOOPS

Fishtail designs (left) allowed archers to shoot downwards on attackers. Wider designs such as crosses (middle) and circles (right) provided a better view of battlefield targets.

Archimedes had devised yet another weapon to repel the marines, who were fighting from the decks [of the ships]. He had had the walls pierced with large numbers of loopholes at the height of a man, which were about a palm's breadth wide at the outer surface of the walls. Behind each of these and inside the walls were stationed archers with rows of so-called "scorpions," a small catapult which discharged iron darts, and by shooting through these embrasures [holes] they put many of the marines out of action.

Still another defensive device, which like the others would see widespread use in medieval castles, was the portcullis, a heavy latticework gate, usually made of wood and shod with iron for extra strength, that was lowered from above the gateway and helped seal off the entrance to a fortress. The fourth-century B.C. Greek writer Aeneas Tacticus left this description of a version of a portcullis from his own time:

ARCHIMEDES VERSUS THE ROMANS

In this excerpt from his biography of Marcellus, from his famous *Lives*, the first-century A.D. Greek writer Plutarch tells how the great Greek inventor Archimedes unleashed various ingenious weapons against the Roman forces besieging Syracuse in 213–212 B.C.

When the Romans first attacked by sea and land, the Syracusans were struck dumb with terror and believed that nothing could resist the onslaught of such powerful forces. But presently Archimedes brought his engines to bear and launched a tremendous barrage against the Roman army. This consisted of a variety of missiles, including a great volley of stones [thrown by catapults larger and more lethal than any yet invented] which descended upon their target with an incredible noise and velocity. There was no protection against this artillery, and the soldiers were knocked down in swathes and their ranks thrown into confusion. At the same time huge beams were run out from the walls so as to project over the Roman ships: some of them were then sunk by great weights dropped from above, while others were seized at the bows by iron claws . . . hauled into the air by means of counterweights . . . until they stood upright upon their sterns, and then allowed to plunge . . . [until they were] dashed against the steep cliffs and rocks.

If a large number of the enemy come in . . . and you wish to catch them you should have ready above the center of the gateway a gate of the strongest possible timber overlaid with iron. Then when you wish to cut off [part of] the enemy [forces] as they rush in, you should let this drop down and the gate itself will not only as it falls destroy some of them, but will also keep the [rest of] the foe from entering, while at the same time the forces on the wall are shooting at the enemy at the gate.

THE PRACTICAL ROMANS

The Romans, a highly practical and imitative people, adopted many aspects of Greek civilization, and not surprisingly they gained much of their knowledge of fortifications and siege craft from the Greeks. Taking various ideas about architecture, engineering, stonemasonry, and artillery weapons from Greek models, the Romans refined and expanded them, then applied them on a scale often far grander than the world had yet seen. In particular, the techniques the Romans perfected for building large stone structures remained in use for many centuries; and after temporarily falling into disuse in Europe after Rome's fall, many of these ideas were revived, almost unchanged, for the construction of stone castles in the Middle Ages.

Among the most important of these techniques were methods of lifting extremely massive stone blocks and other heavy loads to great heights. Some of the stones used in Rome's great sports arena, the Colosseum, for example, were fifteen feet long, weighed five to six tons, and needed to be raised to heights of more than a hundred feet. Parts of some medieval castles attained similar heights. Without the hoists and cranes invented and perfected by the Greeks and Romans, therefore, great structures such as the Colosseum and most medieval castles could never have been erected.

The most common type of hoist used by ancient and medieval builders was the "sheerlegs," here described by engineering historian Donald Hill:

Two stout spars [wooden poles] were held apart at the top by a short cross-piece; at the bottom a windlass [horizontal drum turned by a crank] was installed on bearings fixed to the legs; the lifting [block-and-]tackle was

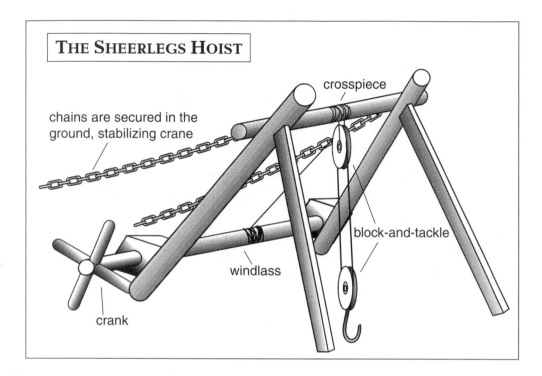

THE SHEERLEGS HOIST

crosspiece

chains are secured in the
ground, stabilizing crane

block-and-tackle

windlass

crank

attached to the cross-piece by a loop of rope. . . . The
rope from the block-and-tackle was wound onto the
drum of the windlass. The crane was held in position by
guy ropes attached to the tops of the spars and into
stakes driven into the ground.

For the heaviest loads, a larger crane was employed. This ingenious and powerful device utilized a circular cage, or drum, in
which several workers operated a treadmill, making the cage
rotate as they walked in place. Recommending the device for
"loads of immense dimensions and weight," the first-century
B.C. Roman architect Vitruvius described it as having a tall
wooden block, or support, surrounded by an elaborate system of
ropes and pulleys. The ends of the ropes, he wrote,

are carried back on the outside of the upper block and
are taken over its lower pulleys, and return below. They
are passed from the inside to the pulleys of the lower
block and are carried up right and left and return to the
top round the highest pulleys. Passing from the outside
they are carried right and left of the drum on the axle,

and are tied so as to hold there. Then another rope is wound round the drum . . . and the drum, being trodden by men, can produce [quick] results.

A sculpted relief of this very machine, with five men operating the treadmill, was discovered in the tomb of the Roman Haterii family, a monument archaeologists have dated to the late first century A.D., the era in which the Colosseum was built.

GREAT FEATS OF MILITARY ENGINEERING

When the Western Roman Empire disintegrated in the fifth and sixth centuries, the Eastern Roman realm, centered at

VITRUVIUS'S INFLUENCE ON LATER AGES

Many of the architectural and engineering devices described by the Roman architect Marcus Vitruvius Pollio (who practiced his craft from about 46 to 30 B.C.) were widely used by medieval builders, although most learned about them indirectly, through craft traditions, rather than directly, by reading his works. Vitruvius was apparently already an old man by the late 20s B.C. when he penned the ten books composing his greatest treatise—*De architectura*, or *On Architecture*. The work covers all types of Greek and Roman building, as well as methods of decoration, mathematics, and diverse aspects of civil engineering. Book One deals with the qualifications of an architect and with town planning; Book Two covers building materials, including brick and concrete; Book Three describes temple architecture; Book Four, the three decorative orders of columns; Book Five, public buildings and how sound propagates within them; Book Six, private dwellings; Book Seven, interior decorations; Book Eight, aqueducts and water systems; Book Nine, geometry, astronomy, and measuring; and Book Ten, mechanics and mechanical devices, including catapults and other war machines. After Rome's fall, *De architectura* survived in various medieval handwritten copies. The edition published in 1486 became a sudden sensation among European architects and established the neoclassical building style that dominated Europe for centuries to come and even influenced American architects such as Thomas Jefferson.

Constantinople on the Bosporus (a narrow strait on the southern edge of the Black Sea), survived and became known as the Byzantine Empire. The early Byzantines preserved and very effectively utilized Roman knowledge of fortifications and siege warfare. The renowned, highly productive Byzantine emperor Justinian (reigned 527–565) strengthened many of the older Roman forts in his realm and built several new ones, completing over seven hundred military works in all. Typical was the castle at Dara, on his empire's eastern border, which had two massive curtain walls, the inner one sixty feet high and studded with hundred-foot-high towers. In many respects it was similar to a number of the large castles the English king Edward I erected in Wales some seven centuries later, when European castle building was at its height.

Perhaps the most impressive of Byzantine fortifications were the defensive walls of Constantinople itself, which kept this great city safe from invaders for hundreds of years. John Warry provides this excellent concise description:

> The outer face of the fortifications was protected by a broad, deep moat. An attacker who overcame this obstacle would then be confronted by a breastwork [fortifica-

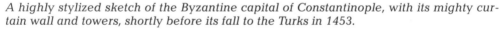

A highly stylized sketch of the Byzantine capital of Constantinople, with its mighty curtain wall and towers, shortly before its fall to the Turks in 1453.

tion] approximately equal to his own height, and some 40 feet behind this, as an inner defense, stood a chain of towers, linked by a curtain wall 26 feet high. The fourth line of defense was the main city wall itself, lying back at a further distance of 66 feet, 43 feet in height, and fortified by great towers from which . . . showers of missiles could be directed into the flanks [sides] of the assailants. Other walls of solid masonry defended the perimeter of the city where it was adjacent to the sea. These embraced the whole headland and connected with the land walls at either end.

These defenses rank among the greatest feats of military engineering of all time. Along with other examples of major Greek and Roman fortifications that survived into the Middle Ages, they could not fail to impress early medieval builders charged with creating effective defenses for their own rulers. As Sidney Toy says, it was largely to these powerful ancient works, "many of which still exist, that the medieval military engineer . . . owed his inspiration."

BASTIONS OF UNCHALLENGED POWER: THE DEVELOPMENT OF MEDIEVAL CASTLES

Despite the fact that the construction, layout, and features of ancient fortifications influenced medieval builders, the transition from ancient to medieval European castles was far from smooth and clear-cut. After the breakup of the Western Roman Empire, the "barbarian" kingdoms that grew on its wreckage were, for several centuries, often politically disorganized or unstable and, by Greek and Roman standards, culturally and scientifically backward. As a result, many of the surviving Roman forts were either allowed to fall into ruin or scavenged of their stones to erect smaller, less impressive structures. Architectural historian Peter Kidson cites the example of Britain, abandoned by Roman troops to the Angles, Saxons, and other Germanic tribes in the fifth century:

> Nearly all those vestiges of a comparatively highly organized way of life in Roman Britain which were not destroyed outright seem to have been treated by the newcomers with the disdain of incomprehension. Buildings such as baths, temples, basilicas, and theaters lay wholly beyond the range of their experience. Moreover, the pattern of settlement changed over the entire country. Many Roman towns and nearly all the Roman country villas were totally abandoned; so that from the Anglo-Saxon point of view perhaps the most important aspect of Roman buildings was the facility with which they could be exploited for building material.

For a long time, therefore, European forts remained essentially like the *oppida* described by the famous Roman general Julius Caesar when he invaded Gaul, what is now France, in the 50s B.C. A Germanic *oppidum* was a hill fort consisting of high, massive banks of earth strengthened by piled layers of timber and fieldstones. "From a practical point of view," Caesar wrote, this style was "very useful for the defense of cities. The stone gives protection from fire and the wood resists battering-rams."

EARLY EUROPEAN CASTLES

It is uncertain how much these primitive yet strong and relatively effective hill forts influenced the development of the first medieval castles in western Europe; what *is* certain is that by the tenth century the lords of western Germany, Denmark, and especially Normandy, along the English Channel in northern France, were building the first "motte-and-bailey" castles. A motte was a conical hill varying from 10 to 100 feet in height and from 100 to 300 feet in diameter. The summit of the motte was protected by a wooden stockade, or palisade, probably

In this more advanced version of a Norman motte-and-bailey castle, the original wooden stockades that topped the motte and surrounded the bailey have been replaced by more formidable stoneworks.

made of boards or logs jammed vertically into the earth and braced by one or more rows of horizontal boards running around the perimeter. Just below the motte, and also protected by a stockade, were one or more baileys (or wards), spacious open areas in which people, as well as horses, pigs, and sheep, could find quarter when an enemy threatened the surrounding territory. The twelfth-century French writer Jean de Colmieu described other features of such forts:

> It is the custom . . . [to] dig a ditch about [the motte] as wide and deep as possible. . . . Inside the enclosure is a citadel, or keep, which commands the whole circuit of the defenses. The entrance to the fortress is by means of a bridge, which, rising from the outer side of the moat and supported on posts as it ascends, reaches to the top of the mound.

The general design of a motte-and-bailey allowed for defenders to fight first from behind the outer stockade(s) that ringed the bailey(s); and if need be, when this barrier was breached, to retreat to the citadel atop the motte. The upper defenses were more formidable, partly because their high vantage gave a clear view of enemy movements and, more importantly, because the attackers faced the difficult task of advancing uphill, while arrows, rocks, and other missiles rained down on them.

However, a motte-and-bailey's best defenses were only effective in the short run, for the people confined in the cramped space inside the upper enclosure could not hold out for long periods. As medieval scholar John Burke describes it, "Permanent residence at the top of the mound was neither easy nor desirable. There was little room to move about, sanitary conditions must have been deplorable, and it was a daunting task to carry food up from below and maintain adequate stocks in preparation for an emergency." During a siege it was, of course, impossible to acquire fresh supplies and the prospect of starvation no doubt led to surrender on many an occasion.

THE NORMAN CONQUEST

A great flurry of castle building occurred in the eleventh century after the Normans invaded England. On or about October 14, 1066, the powerful Norman lord known to posterity as William the Conqueror, having crossed the English Channel, crushed

A BARBARIAN FORTRESS

When the Roman general Julius Caesar invaded Gaul in the 50s B.C., he witnessed firsthand the impressive hill forts constructed by the natives, who belonged to one of the successive waves of Germanic peoples that had spread across northern Europe and whom the Greeks and Romans collectively referred to as "barbarians." In his *Commentaries on the Gallic War* (translated by Rex Warner), Caesar gave this description of one such fortress:

A Gallic warrior stands before a "barbarian" timber hill fort.

> Beams of timber are laid on the ground at intervals of two feet all along the length of the wall and at right angles to it. The beams are then fastened together on the inside and banked up with a good lot of earth; the intervals between them are fitted in with larger stones facing outward. When this course has been laid and the beams tightly fastened together, another course is laid on top of it. This is arranged so that, while the same interval is maintained between the beams, those of the second course are not in contact with those of the first, but are laid on a layer of stones two feet high. . . . Course is added to course in the same way until the wall reaches the required height. This is an agreeable style of building to look at. . . . It is also, from a practical point of view, a style that is very useful for the defense of cities. The stone gives protection from fire and the wood resists battering-rams.

the Anglo-Saxons at the Battle of Hastings. King Harold II, the leader of the native defenders, died that day along with two of his brothers and most of England's best soldiers. Further opposition was minimal, and William was able to assert nearly complete military domination of the country. In fact, it was the lack of strong native English castles that contributed most to the ease of the Norman Conquest; and conversely, William's subsequent very vigorous campaign of castle building ensured that his control of the land would be effective and permanent.

William the Conqueror (on horse in foreground) oversees the landing of his troops in southern England in the early autumn of 1066.

Naturally enough, the first Norman castles on English soil were motte-and-baileys. The first large version was that constructed at Berkhamsted, twenty-five miles northwest of London, in the late autumn of 1066, to help secure the latter town's surrender. But these structures proved, for the most part, to be stopgap measures, for their builders recognized early on that their wooden gates and stockades were susceptible to fire damage; so the Normans began replacing the wooden enclosures with stone walls.

The result was a "shell keep," basically a single circular wall enclosing an inner bailey atop a hill. Typically, small living quarters, workshops, stables, and storerooms lined the inside of the wall, their doors opening into the bailey. In more advanced versions, stone towers—or inner keeps, which were usually substantially taller than the outer walls—were erected in the centers of the baileys. The shell keep at Restormel, in English Cornwall, large sections of which have survived, is an excellent example. The main shell wall is surrounded by a wide, deep moat. Within the shell itself is another ring wall, concentric to the first, surrounding a circular inner court, the distance between the two ring walls being just over eighteen feet. In that space, cross-walls create separate rooms and apartments, most two stories high. Originally located on the ground floor were the cellars, for storing food and arms; the upper floor contained the living quarters; and the kitchen, located near the gateway, occupied both floors. Restormel's well-ordered circular structure is broken in only one spot, a point on the northeastern section of the rim, by a square tower projecting outward. The tower was originally intended for defensive purposes but was later converted to a chapel.

A Norman stone keep rises inside the innermost of three curtain walls, each of which is studded by massive towers and encloses a bailey.

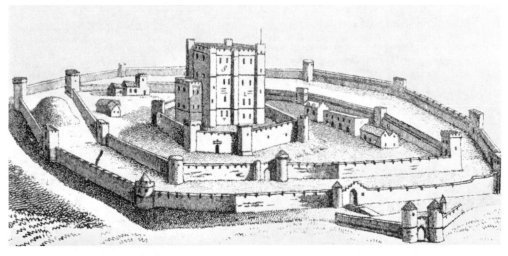

Construction techniques for shell keeps were fairly straightforward and uncomplicated. Although the noble owners of these early castles dictated their location and overall layout, it was the local stonemasons and carpenters who did the actual work; and these craftsmen used methods based partly on traditions, passed on from one generation of builders to another, from earlier cultures. Most commonly, flat rectangular stones or bricks were piled on top of one another in the age-old manner; however, some slightly more sophisticated masonry styles were used for parts of many shell keeps. The most prominent example is herringbone masonry, here explained by Sidney Toy:

> In herringbone masonry the material comprising each course, flat stones or bricks, is laid, not horizontally, but tilted up about 45 degrees. Bond is obtained by tilting the stones in each succeeding course in the reverse direction to that below it, and sometimes further by the insertion of one horizontal line between the courses. . . .

In this modern engraving by W. B. Scott, English workers toil in the construction of a new castle in about 1080. Note the use of scaffolding consisting of wooden timbers lashed together with ropes.

THE SHELL KEEP AT LAUNCESTON

In this excerpt from his book *Castles: Their Construction and History*, noted scholar Sidney Toy describes the shell keep at Launceston, in the southwestern English district of Cornwall. It was originally built as a motte-and-bailey in about 1080; the shell wall was added about a century later and the inner tower about 1240.

The keep at Launceston is composed of an ovoid-shaped [egg-shaped] shell and a round tower . . . inside the shell. Here the shell . . . is 12 ft. thick and 30 ft. high, and has a deep battered plinth [course of foundation stones] crowned by a round molding. The wall walk was reached by two mural stairways, one near the gateway and one on the opposite side of the keep. . . . The keep is approached up the steep mound, which investigation has proved to be a natural hillock [some mottes were artificially constructed], by a long flight of steps, formerly flanked by walls and covered in by a roof. The foot of the stairway was guarded by a round tower, and at the head stood the . . . entrance to the keep which was later protected by a portcullis [a wooden grille strengthened by iron]. . . . Considering its commanding position, its three lines of defense, and its magnificent middle platform [inner tower], this keep when complete must have been amongst the most formidable in England.

Two courses of such work present much the appearance of the bones of a herring. This method of construction is not of itself conclusive evidence of any particular period. It was used by the Romans [across Europe] and the Saxons [in pre-Norman England], and was employed extensively by the Normans.

With their combinations of regular and herringbone stonemasonry, Norman shell keeps like those built in southwestern England at Restormel, Totnes (in Devon), and Launceston (in Cornwall) constituted an important evolutionary link between earthen and wooden hill forts and full-fledged medieval stone castles.

CASTLES IN THE FEUDAL ORDER

The Norman Conquest introduced into England not only a widespread system of castles, but also a social system intimately connected to these military strongholds. Motte-and-baileys, shell keeps, and other early Norman castles both reflected and strengthened the new feudal social order that had spread across most of Europe in the eighth through eleventh centuries. One scholar describes this order as one in which "a free man provided [a] noble with the military services of himself and his followers in exchange for the tenure of land." Owning and exploiting land, then, was the principal motive that drove the system; and such ownership and exploitation translated into wealth, prestige, and power. Indeed, society became increasingly localized in character, with petty kings, princes, dukes, barons, and other nobles exercising great power over their own small kingdoms or large estates. Castles were the key to this power, for the nobles could not have maintained power without strong centralized forts to protect their holdings and safely house themselves, their leading followers, and their military weapons and supplies. Thus, the larger and more impregnable castles became, the more easily their owners could maintain control over European life and institutions.

Medieval lords and ladies enjoy a castle's grounds in this illustration from the Book of Hours.

A brief examination of how the feudal system worked reveals that it not only depended in large degree on castles, but also influenced the steady and widespread proliferation of these structures. A lord and his loyal soldiers and followers, called vassals (or retainers), cemented their bond in a solemn public ceremony of "homage," a term derived from the French word for man—*homme*—signifying that the vassal was to become the lord's "man." Noted scholars of the period Clara and Richard Winston explain:

> The vassal "commended" himself to his lord . . . placing his hands in the lord's hands and swearing fealty [loyalty]. Essentially a pact was made, with the vassal under-

taking certain fixed obligations, especially to defend the lord with his body. In return the lord promised protection and economic maintenance. . . . When the lord was an important chieftain, he had great lands to give away to his comrades in arms. . . . [The vassals], in their turn, had far more land than they could properly exploit or hold. . . . They could distribute the land among others who in their turn were subvassals. Periodically the lord sent word to his vassals, reminding them of their duty to him. They in turn rallied their men, each of whom brought their dependents . . . for counsel, training, or warfare.

Thus, as time went on, some of a lord's vassals ended up with their own substantial lands. Having become lords in their own right, some of these men built castles on their newly acquired lands, strongholds that, ironically, eventually allowed them to compete for power with their former lords. Since every lord needed vassals and some of these vassals inevitably ended up gaining estates of their own, the process often tended to repeat itself. And the result was that more and more castles dotted the countryside. What kept the process from getting completely out of control was the prestige and power of the loftiest

THE CEREMONY OF HOMAGE

This firsthand account of an homage ceremony that took place in Flanders (what is now western Belgium and northern France) in 1127 was set down by the medieval chronicler Galbert of Bruges (quoted in Brian Tierney's *The Middle Ages*, volume 1).

On Thursday the seventh of April, homages were again made to the count being completed in the following order of faith and security. First they did their homage thus, the count asked if he [the vassal] was willing to become completely his man, and the other replied, "I am willing"; and with clasped hands, surrounded by the hands of the count, they were bound together by a kiss. Secondly, he who had done homage gave his fealty to the representative of the count in these words, "I promise on my faith that I will in future be faithful to count William, and will observe my homage to him completely against all persons in good faith and without deceit," and thirdly, he took his oath to this upon the relics of the saints.

lords, especially the king. When they deemed it necessary, they could rally their thousands of vassals and subvassals to put down an unruly, threatening, or rebellious lord. Such local police actions, so to speak, were the motivation for many medieval castle sieges.

On the other hand, the power inherent in castle ownership and the threat of sieges could be turned the opposite way—against the king himself. The fact is that early medieval kings were not all-powerful monarchs; rather, their authority rested on the allegiance of their vassals, who could and sometimes did gang up to make kings do their bidding. The most famous example occurred in 1215 when England's leading lords, unhappy about King John's new tax policies, forced him to sign the

King John signs the Magna Carta, or "Great Charter," in 1215, guaranteeing his vassals basic rights. This concession soon led to the formation of a council of nobles, which eventually developed into the powerful English Parliament.

DUTIES OF MILITARY SERVICE

This version of a vassal's obligation of military service (quoted in Eugen Weber's *The Western Tradition*) dates from late-thirteenth-century France.

> The baron and all vassals of the king are bound to appear before him when he shall summon them, and to serve him at their own expense for forty days and forty nights, with as many knights as each one owes; and he is able to extract from them these services when he wishes and when he has need of them. And if the king wishes to keep them more than forty days at their own expense, they are not bound to remain if they do not wish it. And if the king wishes to keep them at his expense for the defense of the realm, they are bound to remain. And if the king wishes to lead them outside of the kingdom, they need not go unless they wish to, for they have already served their forty days and forty nights.

Magna Carta, an agreement guaranteeing them certain basic rights that even a king could not curtail. John had little choice but to sign. He knew that these vassals could, from their formidable castle strongholds, stage considerably effective offensive and defensive maneuvers against their neighbors, including him. His own castle and resources were little more formidable than those of any one of them, and without the support of their majority, he had no way to enforce his authority.

Another function of castles in the feudal order was to house some of the subvassals on whose service the lords depended. The most important of these retainers were the knights, whose lives, like those of their lord, often revolved around his castle (or castles). They were bound, through their oath, to provide him with a set number of days (most commonly about forty) of cavalry service or castle guard each year. In wartime, they were often expected to serve sixty or more days and to provide horses, arms, and supplies at their own expense. Motte-and-baileys and shell keeps, which generally had limited living spaces, probably provided little more than temporary quarters for a handful of knights—perhaps no more than half a dozen (except during sieges, when many more knights and common folk crowded inside). Later, when castles became much larger, as many as twenty to fifty knights might have permanent quarters in their lord's abode. Castles supporting garrisons of hundreds or even thousands of knights—the most outstanding example being the Krak of the Knights in Palestine—were highly unusual.

CONTROL OF THE LOCAL POPULATION

While castles acted as the administrative and defensive nuclei of the feudal order that controlled society, another, and closely related, social order supported the castles themselves. Since most members of the nobility felt themselves above doing menial work, the lords and their vassals required cheap laborers to grow their food and to maintain their manors. The poor rural peasants who made up the bulk of the population in medieval times were the natural choice; and the exploitation of their labor became the chief facet of the manorial system, a vital prop helping to hold up the larger feudal framework. Without the manorial system, castles, especially large ones, would have been too expensive to maintain and would therefore have been far fewer in number.

On a typical manor, in exchange for a lord's protection, a group of peasants became his serfs, agricultural workers tied to his land and bound to serve him for life. Typically, a lord provided a serf with from four to forty acres of land to farm, usually near and easily accessible to the manor's castle, along with the rights to draw water from his springs and wells and to gather wood from his forests. In exchange, the serf agreed to work a prescribed number of days on the lord's land or in his castle and also to give him some of the crops raised on his own land. "For instance," writes medieval historian Marjorie Rowling,

> one serf gave his lord a bushel of wheat, 18 sheaves of oats, three hens and one cock each year and five eggs at Easter. In addition he had to work three days in every week for the lord, except at Christmas, Easter and Whitsuntide [or White Sunday, the seventh Sunday after Easter], when he had a week free.

Life for serfs, and poor free laborers as well, was usually hard and monotonous. Each autumn they sowed wheat and rye; and each spring they planted other grains, along with legumes; then, in the summer, they harvested both crops. Between these times of backbreaking work, they performed

During the September harvest peasants pick grapes in the shadow of their lord's imposing castle.

dozens of lesser but equally demanding chores, including maintaining, repairing, and/or resupplying their lord's castle and its grounds. With few exceptions, a peasant's life was also highly restricted and narrow. "His whole world," another noted scholar, Anne Fremantle, points out, "his village, the manor-house [castle], the surrounding fields and woods—might encompass less than two square miles."

A peasant shears a sheep in a drawing from a fifteenth-century manuscript.

Thus, with both vassals and peasants dependent on and owing them heavy obligations, the masters of early medieval castles wielded widespread and feared authority; and, thereby, from these bastions of power, they controlled society. "Not only could a castle block invasion of a region," say the Gieses, "but it could also provide effective control over the local population. Both aspects of the castle were well understood in . . . Europe, where the owners of castles were soon unchallenged owners of power." Yet, as extensive as that power was at the time of the Norman Conquest, it would soon become far larger and more formidable. Even as William and his immediate heirs were tightening their grip on England, new construction ideas and techniques were making their way across Europe from the Near East, the birthplace of stone fortresses. The day of the classic massive medieval castle, a lasting monument to feudal power, was about to dawn.

3

From Crusaders to Stonemasons: Planning and Building the Outer Defenses

By the end of the year 1066, a few months after William of Normandy led his soldiers across the English Channel and overpowered the native inhabitants, England could boast no more than half a dozen castles, probably all of them timber motte-and-baileys. In contrast, by the turn of the twelfth century, slightly over three decades later, more than five hundred castles brooded over the English countryside. This represents an average of a castle every ten miles or so. Most of these, too, were constructed of wood, although the Normans steadily converted them to stone shell keeps or even larger masonry structures.

The rapid encastellation of, or introduction and spread of castles through, England in the late eleventh century was mirrored in northern France and northern Germany. As a result, in the following century these three regions, together making up the "central western European area," remained militarily more advanced and formidable than most of the rest of Europe. During the twelfth century and on into the thirteenth, the castle-building trend continued and in fact quickly accelerated. Many hundreds of castles appeared in this period in the British Isles alone. Castles became not only more numerous, but also much larger, more complex, and stronger, both physically and strategically. These sweeping changes—which in the course of about two centuries covered most of Europe with a dense network of powerful stone fortifications—are most easily traced in the development and improvement of the outer defenses of these

41

structures. Effective protection and defense were, after all, the principal purposes of the medieval castle.

THE SPREAD OF NEW MILITARY TECHNOLOGY

These developments and improvements in European castles were in large degree motivated by increasing contacts with the lands of the eastern Mediterranean, especially the Byzantine Empire and Palestine, distinguished by their long tradition of building elaborate stone fortifications. In 1096 a number of European kings and lords responded to the pleas of Pope Urban II to go to Palestine and liberate Christian holy sites from Muslim control. One important result of this first of the several so-called Crusades that spanned the late eleventh through fourteenth centuries was that Christian knights were impressed by and immediately began to copy the Eastern forts they encountered. According to Frances and Joseph Gies:

European knights swarm out of a siege tower and onto the battlements of Jerusalem during the First Crusade in 1099. Some of these knights brought Eastern military technology back to Europe.

Of the peasants and knights who tramped or sailed to the Holy Land and survived the fighting, most soon returned home. The defense of the conquered territory was therefore left to a handful of knights—primarily the new military brotherhoods, the Templars and the Hospitallers. Inevitably their solution was the same as that of William the Conqueror, but the castles they built were from the start large, of complex design, and of stone. The crusaders made use of the building skills of their sometime Greek allies and their Turkish enemies, improved by their own experience. The results were an astonishing leap forward to massive, intricately designed fortresses of solid masonry.

Among the crusaders' principal Eastern influences were the enormous and sophisticated walls and towers protecting the Byzantine cities of Constantinople (the empire's capital), Nicaea, and Antioch. As they marched through Asia Minor, what is now Turkey, on their way to Palestine, the Europeans also saw seemingly impregnable Byzantine stone castles sited at strategic points in the countryside. These forts quartered garrisons of horse and foot soldiers on a full-time basis, forces that could swiftly move out and intercept an enemy force attempting to penetrate imperial territory.

In addition to learning strategic lessons about castles, the crusaders also borrowed design and construction ideas. An example of a specific feature they copied from Byzantine models was machicolation, the outward projection of a wall at the top of the battlements; missiles or boiling oil could be dropped through openings in the floors of such projections onto attackers. Machicolation was essentially the stone version of wooden hoardings, platforms, often roofed for protection, that rested on horizontal timbers projecting outward from holes near the tops of fortifications. Stone machicolation, which was not susceptible to fire damage as hoardings were, soon became common in castles throughout Europe (although hoardings continued in use in older castles well into the fourteenth century). Among other castle features that spread from the East to the West was the portcullis, the heavy vertical gateway door used extensively by the ancient Greeks and Romans. Such doors were usually made of thick wood reinforced with iron shodding and moved up and

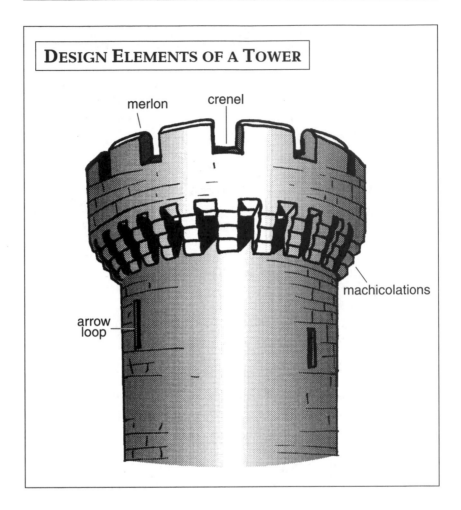

DESIGN ELEMENTS OF A TOWER

merlon   crenel

machicolations

arrow loop

down via chains attached to a winch operated from a small chamber above the main gates.

Arrow loops, like those employed by Archimedes in the defense of ancient Syracuse, were another popular feature introduced from the East. Bearing the medieval nickname of "murderesses," these narrow vertical wall slits allowed castle archers to shoot repeated volleys of arrows at approaching enemy troops. In principal, arrow loops were similar to crenellation, the succession of notches at the tops of battlements, a feature already long employed in European castles. Defending archers alternated at hiding behind the merlons and firing through the crenels. Arrow loops had a design advantage that made them even more effective than crenellation, namely that on the outside, the loops

THE ADVANTAGES OF PROJECTING TOWERS

Towers, both squared and rounded, projecting outward from a curtain wall gave a castle certain extra defensive advantages. In this excerpt from his book *Crusader Castles*, scholar Robin Fedden discusses these advantages and the evolution of such towers.

The transition from the square tower in the curtain wall to the round tower has been claimed as an important milestone in the development of military architecture. . . . In fact, the important change in the design of towers was not from the square to the round tower, but in the extent to which towers projected beyond the curtain wall. Towers have a variety of uses, but their *raison d'être* [essential purpose] is to provide flanking fire [arrows and other missiles aimed at the sides of the enemy force]. Whatever method of attack is used, the besieger must approach close to the castle walls. Towers of bold projection enable the defenders to enfilade [shoot at the enemy's whole battle line] from advantageous positions with slings, arrows, and other missiles. They give to the besieged the possibility of conducting an active defense and seriously discouraging the besiegers, a matter of some importance for the morale of a garrison. . . . Consequently design progressed from towers of small projection at long intervals to boldly projecting towers set comparatively close together. If there is an equal salient [amount of projection], there is not much to choose between a round and a square tower. Round towers are less vulnerable to bombardment and mining, and they provide a better field of fire. On the other hand, square towers may have been more convenient for the operation of medieval artillery [catapults and so on].

The formidable cluster of crenellated towers protecting this Italian castle provided its defenders with a wide field of fire against attackers.

This twelfth-century French castle displays numerous arrow loops and square holes for attaching wooden hoardings.

presented a very narrow, difficult target to attackers; while on the inside, they flared outward, giving the defenders plenty of room to move around and command a wide field of fire. Throughout the twelfth century, European builders employed arrow loops on new castles and added them to existing ones.

Although the most powerful lords of France, Germany, and England fairly quickly adopted the military technologies they learned, from both contacts with the Near East and their own experience, these new ideas tended to spread more slowly to other, less advanced sectors of Europe. As medieval historian Robert Bartlett explains, one way they spread was through conquest.

> The knights and castle-builders and crossbowmen of the central western European area used their military might to extend their lordship into the lands of the east and west. Norman expansion in the British Isles and German conquests in eastern Europe both involved the arrival of new military methods and new weapons in the conquered areas. The second way that technology spread was a direct consequence of the first. As the aggressive forces threatened the supremacy of native rulers . . . these countered in the most effective way—by imitation. By the mid–thirteenth century the rulers of, for instance, Wales [the region encompassing most of western Britain]

. . . had become virtually indistinguishable from their foes in armament and methods of waging war. . . . In these ways . . . the techniques and methods of England, France, and Germany gradually reached the whole of the Latin West . . . over the course of the twelfth, thirteenth and early fourteenth centuries.

COSTLIER BUT MORE EFFECTIVE DEFENSES

Thanks to the spread of new military technology, the full-fledged castles erected in Europe in the twelfth and thirteenth centuries exhibited many important political, physical, and strategic differences from the quickly outmoded motte-and-baileys. A major political-economic difference was that motte-and-baileys had been relatively easy and inexpensive to build. For example, the Normans had built two complete forts of this variety in the two-week interval between their landing in England and the showdown at Hastings. By contrast, a more advanced stone castle like that at Dover (in southeastern England), built by King Henry II in the late twelfth century, took several decades to complete.

Dover Castle was also extremely expensive to erect, and similar large castles became progressively more costly. Henry spent an estimated 6,500 English pounds on Dover between 1168 and 1189, and his overall expenditure on castles averaged 700 pounds per year; his son John spent perhaps 1,000 pounds a year on castle building; John's son, Henry III, spent at least 1,500 pounds per year; and Henry III's eldest son, the great castle builder Edward I (reigned 1272 to 1307), outdid all of his predecessors with an outlay of more than 80,000 pounds in twenty-seven years just on the castles he constructed in Wales. In 1296 Edward employed over 2,600

Conway Castle, built on the River Conway between 1283 and 1287 by King Edward I, is defended by eight massive stone towers.

workmen in the final stages of construction on Conway Castle, spending up to 250 pounds a week. It is uncertain what these sums would translate into in modern money; however, their enormity can be illustrated by the fact that at that time a knight on campaign made about three pounds a month; and this was at least seventy times more than a common laborer's monthly earnings.

The new military technology was also characterized by a more strategic selection of sites for castles and more scientific planning of the outer defenses. Whenever possible, new castles were built with their backs at the edges of very steep hills, ideally rocky cliffs having high vertical walls, thus making it virtually impossible to mount an attack from the rear. Sidney Toy elaborates and cites a well-known example:

> The main defense was concentrated in the direction of approach, and here there were often two or even three lines of advance fortifications. . . . In the case of castles already built, one or two outer baileys [each with its own protective curtain wall] were added on the line of approach. . . . Among the first of these castles was the Chateau Gaillard [in Normandy], which stands on a precipitous cliff 300 ft. above the river Seine. It was built by [England's] Richard I and when complete in 1198 was one of the most powerful castles of the day. . . . The castle consists of three baileys, arranged in a line, the inner bailey being on the edge of the cliff. The outer bailey . . . was completely surrounded by a moat; and there was a moat between the middle and inner baileys. The curtains of both the outer and middle baileys were strengthened by circular wall towers. . . . The keep, or donjon, stands on the edge of the precipice, principally within but partially projecting outside the inner bailey, where its base rises up from a ledge of rock 40 ft. below the level of the courtyard.

ELIMINATING THE "DEAD GROUND"

That Château-Gaillard's keep was roughly circular in shape reflected another recent advance in defensive strategy. In the eleventh century, when motte-and-baileys and shell keeps still predominated in Europe, French castle builders introduced rectangular keeps; and shortly after conquering England, the Normans built several of these in that country, one famous example being the White Tower in London. Unfortunately, as experience soon proved, rectangular keeps had some significant disadvantages. First, their corners were particularly vulnerable to sappers, or miners, who dug tunnels beneath the walls, causing them to sink; and also to battering rams. Both sappers and rams often attempted to take advantage of the "dead ground," the area directly in front of a corner and equidistant from its two side walls; this was because defensive fire from within the keep had great difficulty reaching the dead grounds at the four corners.

This problem was significantly alleviated by an idea crusaders brought back from the Near East—circular or multiangular (for instance, octagonal) keeps. These keeps presented no dead ground to shield attackers and therefore allowed for a more flexible and effective concentration of defensive fire. Such keeps differed from the earlier shell keeps, which were also circular, in two ways. First, the later versions were generally much larger and more complex. Second, rather than standing in the center of a single, cramped bailey at the top of a mound, the new circular keeps were most often sited within the innermost of several large, open baileys, each protected by its own ring of imposing walls. Château-Gaillard's keep, resting inside the innermost bailey, is one prominent example; Pembroke Castle, built in the 1190s in Wales, is one of many others.

Other features that improved and strengthened castle defenses included improved versions of two very old ideas—drawbridges and barbicans, both designed to defend a castle's main gate. A drawbridge was a wooden plat-

The battlements of the White Tower in London, a rectangular keep erected in 1080 (and later significantly renovated), stand some ninety feet above the ground.

form that spanned the moat and that could be drawn back in an emergency, forcing attackers to enter the moat in order to reach the gate. Early versions simply slid back from the moat and remained in a horizontal position on the ground in front of the gate. Later, chains were attached to the outer ends of the bridge and, by means of chains and winches, retracted into a chamber over the gate; when the chains were fully retracted, the bridge stood vertically against the face of the gate, creating an additional barrier to penetration. Other versions used various arrangements of pivots and counterweights to raise and lower the bridge.

A medieval barbican, like ancient versions seen at Troy and numerous other stone citadels, was an outwork or forward extension of the gate's walls, often forming an outer walled enclosure. Sometimes a barbican had its own fortified gate. As in Troy's eastern defenses, the tactical advantage of such an enclosure was that attackers first had to enter it before they could reach the main gate; and once inside the barbican, they were subjected to a deadly rain of missiles from the battlements at the tops of its walls. Some of the more elaborate castles had multiple barbicans. A notable example is Conway Castle, built by Edward I in northern Wales; both the eastern and western gates are screened by lofty barbicans, one with its own strong gate and drawbridge.

SKILL, PATIENCE, AND BACKBREAKING LABOR

Not surprisingly, the huge and incredibly strong and durable walls, keeps, battlements, barbicans, and other features of a medieval castle's outer defenses required both great skill and much backbreaking labor to construct. A number of different kinds of

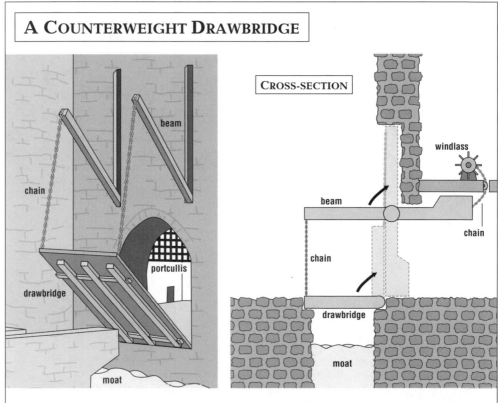

A COUNTERWEIGHT DRAWBRIDGE

CROSS-SECTION

beam

windlass

chain

beam

chain

chain

portcullis

drawbridge

chain

drawbridge

moat

moat

Some castle drawbridges operated by means of counterweights. The wooden drawbridge normally rested over the moat. To raise the bridge, defenders allowed the heavy rear ends of large beams to fall. As the lighter front ends rose, they raised the bridge by means of chains connecting the two.

This drawing from a fifteenth-century manuscript shows masons, wrights, and smiths building a castle atop a rocky, easily defended crag.

specialized craftsmen, as well as dozens, and at times hundreds, of ordinary laborers, worked off and on for years to erect the average castle. Because most of the defenses were made of stone, stonemasons were the most important of the craftsmen; and the foremost of these was the "master-mason." The medieval master-mason was often, in modern terms, a combination of architect, building contractor, and general overseer. In most cases, he designed the castle, found and organized the workers, and kept a close eye on all construction stages. Donald Hill here compares some of the primary functions and duties of medieval master-masons to those of their modern counterparts:

> Nowadays the architect prepares a complete set of working drawings and specifications that are transmitted to the builder who is to execute the work. . . . In theory the architect should not need to visit the site, except to deal with contractual matters . . . [or] to deal with unforeseen problems that always arise during the course of construction. . . . In the Middle Ages things were quite different.

THE IMPREGNABLE KRAK OF THE KNIGHTS

In Syria, near what is now the northern border of Lebanon, looms one of the world's foremost surviving examples of medieval military architecture—the Krak des Chevaliers, or Krak of the Knights (the term *krak* deriving from the Arabic word *karak*, meaning "fortress"). This most famous and impressive of the crusader castles was the strongest in the Holy Land and served as a regular launching point for Christian expeditions against the Muslims to its east and south. The design of its defenses also influenced castle building in both the eastern Mediterranean and various parts of Europe.

The krak stood on the site of a Muslim castle, which the crusaders took over in 1110 and largely demolished in constructing their own. It is not difficult to understand why both sides found the site—at the top of a steep spur bordered by rugged ravines on three sides—an ideal location for a fortress. When completed, the krak had two baileys, one within the curtain wall of the other, each having three imposing towers in its south wall. The main gate, protected by a huge moat and a drawbridge, was placed near the end of the east wall, so that to reach it an attacking enemy force had to move nearly two-thirds the length of the castle under direct fire from the battlements. Any attackers who made it to the gate and managed to breach it still faced several formidable defenses. The first of these was a narrow, sloping passageway lined with arrow loops and machicolations, from which the defenders could deliver a lethal rain of missiles. At the end of the passage stood a massive iron-shod portcullis, itself protected by machicolations.

With such effective defensive features, not to mention a garrison of knights numbering an estimated two thousand in the castle's heyday, the seemingly impregnable krak proved an alluring but frustrating target to successive Muslim armies. In the course of sixteen decades, the mighty fortress successfully withstood at least twelve furious sieges; while inside, the knights and peasants from the local countryside lived in reasonable comfort thanks to a plentiful water supply from the castle's well; on-site granaries, bakeries, and oil presses; and even a windmill for grinding corn. When the krak finally fell in 1271 to the Muslim sultan Beibars (or Baybars) I, it was more the result of trickery than military failure. When the use of force failed, the sultan sent the defenders a forged surrender order, supposedly from the knights' grand commander in Tripoli, fifty miles to the southwest. Falling for the ruse, the defenders surrendered, signaling the end of the krak's proudest era.

Drawings were sometimes made, but these were undimensioned illustrations to assist the clients to visualize the appearance of the completed buildings—what we should call artists' impressions. These were not intended to be used for passing on the architect's design to the builders. For this function there was no alternative to the constant supervision of the architect himself. His first task was to set out the ground plan of the building, and supervise the clearance and preparation of the site. In the process of setting out the work, ropes, cords, fir poles and lime were used to mark the boundaries of the building as well as to indicate foundation lines for interior walls and pillars.

Working directly under the master-mason were other types of masons of various grades and specialties. "In order to get the stones prepared for him," architectural historian Hugh Braun explains,

> each master-mason has to employ a team of perhaps up to a dozen stone cutters, or "hewers." These may be of varying grades of skill, from the ax-men who cut plain blocks of walling-stone to the experienced dressers who can, under the master-mason's direction, prepare stones of any shape required. Great accuracy is needed, or the result will be a clumsily-built wall. Unusually-shaped stones for special positions must be within the capabilities of the hewers. . . . From the "lodges" [makeshift workshops] occupied by the stone-cutters, gangs of laborers carried the dressed stone to the position in which it was to be laid; here would be found other masons, known as "setters," who would carefully place the stones on their new beds and set them in their matrix of mortar.

Other skilled craftsmen overseen by the master-mason included carpenters, called "wrights," who made doors and installed roofs and hoardings; "plumbers" (from the Latin word for lead—*plumbum*), who fashioned lead pipes and roof linings; and "smiths," who made and hung hinges and other iron accessories.

That the masons and other workers were able to construct castles of such immense size, complexity, and technical precision is a tribute to their great patience and dedication; for the tools and work-saving devices at their disposal were simple and

MEDIEVAL TOOLS

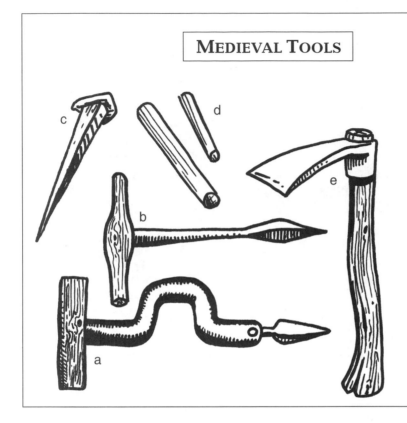

(a) A brace for boring and drilling, invented by medieval wrights; (b) a point for making furrows; (c) a punch for making holes; (d) pegs for joining wooden planks; and (e) an ax, or adze.

even primitive by modern standards. Early European masons used an iron ax for both hewing and dressing stones. By the eleventh century, however, they had begun using a wide chisel called a "bolster," which they struck with a sturdy wooden mallet, the "mell." In most cases, a bolster produced finer, more precise cuts than an ax. The twelfth century brought another slight improvement in the "claw-tool," a bolster with a serrated, or toothed, edge. Masons became so skilled with these implements that the "toolings," the parallel grooves they etched in the stones, often look as if they had been machined.

Once the hewers cut and dressed a batch of stones, the setters laid them in place in a half-finished wall. Work gangs or horse-drawn wagons transported the stones from the hewers to the setters, who stood on wooden scaffolding erected earlier by a team of wrights. Lifting the stones up to the top level of scaffolding was accomplished by some of the same kinds of hoists and cranes described by the Roman writer Vitruvius in his famous architectural treatise, which had survived into medieval times in a number of handwritten copies. Small sheerlegs hoists were common. They were placed on the topmost course of stones and held firmly in place by ropes attached to stakes driven into the ground, preferably on both sides of the wall under construction. For unusually heavy loads, treadmill cranes or hoists with pulley systems attached to teams of horses were employed.

Although a finished castle wall was immensely strong, master-masons learned from experience that one thickness of stones was prone to damage by the largest siege machines. So they adopted the method of building two huge walls several feet apart and filling in the space between with masonry rubble, often mixed with mortar. The massive fortification that resulted—when combined with machicolations, arrow loops, moats, huge gateways with portcullises and drawbridges, barbicans, and other defensive features—made the larger medieval castles nearly impregnable bastions. Of course, enemies invariably attempted to break in anyway; and incredibly, as medieval chronicles of sieges attest, they often succeeded.

4

LIKE A MINIATURE COMMUNITY: A CASTLE'S INNER LIVING SPACES

Although a medieval castle primarily functioned as a military fortress, of almost equal importance was the role it played as its noble owner's administrative center and personal residence. In both peacetime and wartime, especially the latter, castles had to be self-contained and more or less self-sustaining miniature communities. Typically, each was equipped with facilities for sleeping, cooking, eating, bathing, worshiping, holding courts or meetings, storing foodstuffs and other essentials, keeping horses, pigs, and other animals, and so on. And contrary to the popular image of castle interiors as cold, drab, and depressing, furnishings and decorations were often surprisingly colorful and elegant. Indeed, the inner living spaces of large castles built from the twelfth century onward were often quite comfortable by medieval standards (keeping in mind that medieval society knew nothing of central heating, electricity, refrigeration, germs and sanitation, or flush toilets).

THE GREAT HALL

The center of castle life was the "great hall," usually referred to simply as the hall, essentially a large one-room structure with a high ceiling. Here, the lord transacted business, and, along with his relatives and some of his most loyal vassals, slept, ate, and socialized. The concept of the hall apparently originated in the motte-and-baileys. The lord and his family slept in a small one-room wooden building atop the motte, while the kitchen, servants' quarters, stables, and storehouses were located below in the bailey. In the large stone castles of the twelfth through the fourteenth centuries, by contrast, the hall was almost always located within the innermost bailey, usually up against a well-guarded section of the curtain wall. The fully developed hall was made of stone rather than timber and also considerably more complex than the earlier version, with one or more extra stories, each with multiple rooms, added above the main room. The following contemporary description, by French chronicler Lambert of Ardres, is of a transitional hall of the early twelfth century, its layout being unusually elaborate for an early timber version but fairly typical for later stone versions.

> The first story was on the ground level, where there were cellars and granaries and great boxes, barrels, casks, and other household utensils. In the story above were the dwelling and common rooms of the residents, including the larders [food storage], pantry [bread room] and buttery [service area for wine and beer] and the great chamber in which the lord and lady slept. Adjoining this was . . . the dormitory of the ladies in waiting and the children. . . . In the upper story of the house were

An early and comparatively small version of a great hall. In later and larger halls, beds were placed in second-story chambers.

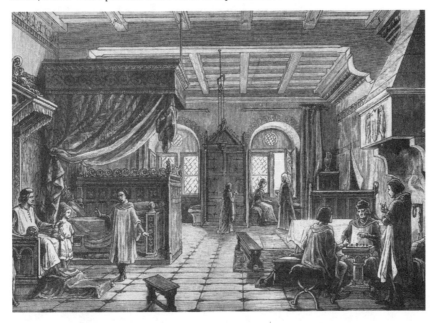

attic rooms in which on the one side the sons of the lord of the house, when they so desired, and on the other side the daughters, because they were obliged, were accustomed to sleep. In this story also the watchmen and the servants appointed to keep the house slept at various times. High up on the east side of the house, in a convenient place, was the chapel. . . . There were stairs and passages from story to story . . . from room to room, and from the house into the gallery, where they used to entertain themselves with conversation, and again from the gallery into the chapel.

Note Lambert's observation that the "dwelling and common rooms" were on the second floor. A few castles had the common, or main, room or rooms on the first floor; but most, for the sake of greater security, placed them on the second floor, reachable by a single well-fortified stairway.

Whether on the first or second floor, the hall's main room was solidly constructed and spacious. Early versions had a central area flanked by an aisle, or wing, on each side, similar to the layout of many churches. This arrangement was dictated by the need to run rows of wooden or stone pillars down the length of the room to support the weight of the massive roof. In time, medieval wrights developed a triangular support called a truss, which enabled them to eliminate the aisles and pillars. The result was a huge and airy open space.

As a rule, this large space was only sparsely furnished with wooden tables and benches. Servants frequently rearranged these, depending on the time of day, the function—meals, meetings, and wedding parties, for example—and the number of people using the area. Carpets were draped on the walls (to help block cold drafts) and on tables and benches; however, carpets were not widely used as floor coverings in the castles of northwestern Europe until the fourteenth century.

Instead, the floors—which in the earliest halls were of hard-packed earth and in later versions, particularly those on the second story, of timber—were customarily strewn with layers of plant matter. Most often used were rushes, marsh plants with hollow or pithy stems (commonly used in weaving baskets); although herbs, including basil, cowslip, sweet fennel, lavender, mints, tansy, and violets were also employed. The choice of so

A medieval bedchamber. Such rooms typically had little furniture but were comfortably decorated with wooden beams, mirrors, paintings, ornate moldings, and colorful linens.

many sweet-smelling varieties was to help mask the unpleasant odors that invariably built up in most halls. As the fifteenth-century Dutch scholar Desiderius Erasmus observed, under the average hall's floors lurked "an ancient collection of beer, grease, fragments, bones, spittle, excrement of dogs and cats and everything that is nasty."

BEDCHAMBERS AND DINING FACILITIES

Sleeping and eating were two of the hall's most essential functions. At first, the sleeping quarters for the lord and his family were located at one end of the hall and separated from the main part of the room by temporary curtains or screens. Over time these quarters became more elaborate, permanent, and private. Their evolution at Chepstow Castle, built in the early 1070s on the river Wye on the Welsh border, serves as a typical example. The original owner, William Fitz Osborn, substituted for the temporary curtains a permanent wooden partition, giving his family privacy from his live-in retainers, who slept in the hall each night (on benches, makeshift mattresses, or the floor). In the thirteenth century, later owners removed the partition, thereby enlarging the hall's main chamber; at the same time, above that end of the hall, they added new sleeping quarters, accessed by a wooden stairway. A few decades later, they extended this upper story across the entire hall, creating a large private suite of rooms. Most castles constructed from the thirteenth century on incorporated such suites from the beginning.

The largest and most important of these personal chambers, used by the lord and lady of the household, was referred to as the solar (pronounced SAW-ler). In time this term came to describe any chamber or apartment located on an upper story. Describing the typical furnishings of such a chamber, Frances and Joseph Gies write:

> Its principal item of furniture was a great bed with a heavy wooden frame and springs made of interlaced ropes or strips of leather, overlaid with a feather mattress, sheets, quilts, fur coverlets, and pillows. Such beds could be dismantled and taken along on the frequent trips a lord made to his other castles and manors. The

The size and splendor of this large fourteenth-century solar are an indication of its owner's great wealth. Note his family crest displayed above the massive fireplace.

THE DEVELOPMENT OF HALL-PORCHES

In this excerpt from his book *An Introduction to English Medieval Architecture*, architectural historian Hugh Braun describes how dealing with the problem of smoke from interior hearths led to the addition of porches on castle and manor-house halls.

> Throughout most of the medieval era the life of the hall centered round the fire burning on its central hearth, whence the smoke, drifting upwards, filled the roof space; to find its way out, eventually, through an aperture in the roof generally protected by a turret or some similar architectural feature. It was nearly always necessary to leave the hall door open if the smoke from the fire was to be allowed to escape. Thus the porch soon became an essential feature in the hall plan; it protected the entrance and greatly added to the comfort of the occupants without obstructing the air supply to the fire. Hall-porches, at first outstripping those of churches, by the Edwardian period [the late thirteenth century] had fallen into line with these; the two-storied church porch of the fifteenth century is frequently to be found repeated in the hall. Some late medieval hall-porches were raised to form what are, in effect, tall towers.

bed was curtained, with linen hangings that pulled back in the daytime and closed at night to give privacy as well as protection from drafts. Personal servants might sleep in the lord's chamber on a pallet or trundle [roll-away] bed, or on a bench. Chests for garments, a few "perches," or wooden pegs, for clothes, and a stool or two made up the remainder of the furnishings.

Although the furniture pieces in such chambers tended to be few in number by today's standards, their dressings were often elegant and comfortable. A surviving inventory of the contents of a late medieval English manor includes:

for the bed in the parlor chamber two pairs of blankets, a pair of sheets, and a red coverlet with green chaplets. Also, a feather bed . . . [and] a green coverlet with pots and ostrich feathers, in the same chamber; a pair of sheets, one pair of blankets and a mattress for the truckle [trundle] bed in the same chamber.

In addition, wall decorations often imparted color and a cozy or refined feeling to a lord and lady's bedchamber. Most walls were either whitewashed, plastered, or paneled and then either hung with paintings or directly embellished with painted designs, flowers being especially popular. The queen's chamber at the White Tower in London, for instance, was decorated with exquisite painted roses. Murals, often highly detailed, were also popular, an outstanding example being the map of the world adorning the hall at Winchester Castle, in southwestern England. Another decoration, painted wool or linen wall hangings, common in early castles, had by the fourteenth century evolved into large, detailed tapestries, which, besides adding a touch of elegance, helped to insulate the cold walls. The walls (or floors) of many solars were also equipped with "squints," small peepholes through which the lord could keep an eye on activities in the hall's main chamber.

The most common of these activities was eating. During meals, the lord's family customarily occupied a wooden or stone dais, or raised platform, at one end of the hall. On the dais rested the main table, which was usually set up and dismantled several times a day; although the wealthiest and most prestigious lords might have "dormant," or permanent, tables. The lord himself sat at a large chair, usually ornately carved and sometimes equipped with a canopy, emphasizing his superior status, while everyone else sat on ordinary benches.

KITCHENS, BATHS, AND TOILETS

Until the fifteenth century, food preparation itself did not as a rule take place in the hall proper. The servants who kept the tables stocked with food and drink hurried to and from a service area behind the "screens," a passageway at the far end of the hall opposite the dais. The buttery, for storing and pouring wine and beer, and the pantry, for storing and slicing bread, were almost always located in this service area. However, the kitchen was located in a separate enclosure outside the hall in the bailey. Castle kitchens in the Middle Ages, constructed at first of timber and later of stone, featured a central stone hearth (later

In this scene from a fifteenth-century French manuscript, servants hurry to accommodate the lady of the castle and her guests while musicians (at upper left) provide entertainment.

several stone fireplaces) for cooking. For special feasts and celebrations, extra makeshift kitchens were erected adjoining the main kitchen, which was often connected to a passageway leading to the screens and the great hall beyond. Usually, the castle garden was planted near the kitchen, giving the cooks easy access to fresh vegetables, fruits, and herbs.

Medieval castles did not have modern-style bathrooms combining bathing and toilet facilities. Instead, baths were taken in a portable wooden tub equipped with a canopy for privacy and filled by servants using buckets; in warm weather a bather might choose a spot in the bailey, while in winter the tub invariably rested near the fireplace in the solar. Some details of a castle lord's bath time are revealed in this excerpt from a manual of servants' duties:

> If your lord wishes to bathe . . . hang sheets round the roof [ceiling], every one full of flowers and sweet green

herbs, and have five or six sponges to sit or lean upon, and a sheet over [the tub] so that he may bathe there a while . . . and always be careful that the door is shut. Have a basin full of hot fresh herbs and wash his body with a soft sponge, rinse him with fair warm rose-water . . . [and then] wipe him dry with a clean cloth.

Those not interested in the full treatment could wash their hands and face at stone basins, one of which was usually located at a central point on each story of the hall. Water entered a basin from a tank above, the tank's water supplied either by servants' buckets or a pipe leading from a cistern, a reservoir for catching rainwater, on the roof.

The toilet, called the "garderobe" or "privy," was in most cases a simple latrine partially hidden in an alcove or recessed area on the outside wall of a chamber. For comfort, some had wooden seats. Less comfortable was the handful of hay that took the place of toilet paper, which had yet to be invented. A long shaft located below the latrine carried wastes to a ditch, the moat, or, in ideal situations, a moving river. However, the odors wafting from these drains, especially in hot weather or during a siege when the castle was crowded, were anything but ideal; and as John Burke remarks, "Sanitation in even the most exalted households left much to be desired." A surviving document tells how, when planning to stay for a while at London's White Tower, King Henry III sent ahead this order:

Since the privy chamber . . . in London is situated in an undue and improper place, wherefore it smells badly, we command you on the faith and love by which you are bounden to us that you in no wise omit to cause another privy chamber to be made . . . in such more fitting and proper place that you may select there, even though it should cost a hundred pounds.

In some castles, the problem was partially solved by diverting rainwater from gutters or cisterns into the latrine shaft, thereby periodically cleaning it out. More often, however, servants known as "gong farmers" were stuck with this unhappy and unhealthy task. Another drawback of latrine drains was the potential for enemy soldiers to infiltrate the castle by climbing through them, as happened at Richard I's Château-Gaillard

THE FALL OF CHÂTEAU-GAILLARD

The danger that a castle's latrine drains posed during a siege became devastatingly clear when, in 1204, France's King Philip II attacked the magnificent Château-Gaillard, which England's King Richard I had built in Normandy a few years before. The castle had three baileys, each protected by a strong curtain wall. Philip's forces had managed to penetrate the outer bailey and were in the midst of their assault on the middle bailey when a French soldier noticed a chapel window in the upper story of a building nestled against the south side of the curtain wall. Reasoning that the building might contain latrines, he led a group of companions along the riverbank in search of the drain outlet. Sure enough, they found it; and one by one they crawled up through it until they reached a point just below the chapel. Once inside the building, the soldiers made a loud racket, giving the impression that a huge force of French had breached the curtain wall. Taking this bait, the defenders set fire to the building and retreated into the inner bailey, unwittingly allowing the tiny band of enemy intruders to hurry to the inside of the gate and lower the drawbridge separating the outer and middle baileys. In this way, the French gained the middle bailey; not long afterward, they managed to take the inner bailey, too, and thereby Château-Gaillard fell into King Philip's grasp.

Château-Gaillard, which fell to the French in 1204 after attackers gained entrance to the middle bailey via a latrine drain.

This view of Saumur Castle in France shows both smaller original windows (at top of gatehouse) and much larger windows added later (in round corner towers).

when France's King Philip II besieged it in 1204. To counter this threat, many builders erected a masonry wall around the outside drain opening.

"ALMOST EVERYTHING YOU NEEDED"

Light and heat were no less important to the comfort of castle dwellers than access to water and toilet facilities. In the daytime, of course, windows provided most of the light. At first, because of concerns for safety in the event of attack, most castle windows were rather small and narrow, and interior chambers tended to be unevenly lit. From the middle of the twelfth century on, however, as castle living spaces grew larger and more comfortable, windows also grew larger, as well as more numerous. The largest window of all was usually located in the hall's main chamber near the lord's dais, providing plenty of light to this focal point of so many of his daily activities. At night, or in the daytime when the window shutters were closed, candles of wax or tallow (melted animal fat) provided light. These were often set in groups in wall brackets or on freestanding iron candleholders, or candelabra. It was not unusual for a large castle to use over a thousand candles per night, often necessitating a candle-making shop on the premises. Oil lamps, either set on a stand or suspended on a chain, and torches set in wall brackets were also common.

CASTLES NOT AS DRAB AS ONCE THOUGHT

For a long time, modern historians assumed that living conditions in the stone halls of medieval castles, which had few of the amenities people take for granted today, were harsh, drab, colorless, and uncomfortable. However, as medieval scholar Dominique Barthélemy here explains, from *Revelations of the Medieval World*, recent research has revealed a surprisingly different picture of castle comforts.

Archaeologists once tended to take the pessimistic view, doubting that such amenities as fireplaces, recessed walls, and latrines were part of the original plan [of castle living spaces]. Recent excavations cast doubt on such skepticism. The beautiful fireplaces found . . . in various eleventh-century halls and the presence of three hearths and two latrines on the second floor of a primitive (eleventh-century) donjon in the castle of Ghent suggest early attempts to increase comfort. . . . As we approach the year 1200 we find pipes supplying water to the upper stories and more elegant wall decorations, as at Ghent, where a sophisticated masonry structure was imitated [in a wall painting]. . . . It takes imagination to visualize the many tapestries that covered these bare walls. . . . There was also a good deal of furniture, which unlike that of today was frequently transported from house to house, as princes and lords together with their entourages made their normal rounds [of various manors]. Admittedly the construction was crude, but drabness and crowding were not as serious as was once thought. . . . It is time to abandon the image of the medieval castle as a "place of sadness."

The heat in early castles came from open hearths, the two most conspicuous resting in the great hall and kitchen. The smoke rose through lanternlike roof turrets that could be open and shut by pulling strings. Over time builders moved these hearths back to and finally into the outer walls, creating the now-familiar fireplaces that have remained common features of homes ever since. Once recessed into walls, fireplaces routinely had funnel-like flues that carried the smoke to chimneys. "The end of the medieval period," Hugh Braun remarks, "saw the romantic turrets of the Gothic [late medieval] heyday replaced with the more practical but still ornamental chimney stack which, surmounted by its clusters of shafts, still provided that element of verticality so sought after by medieval designers."

Windows and fireplaces also became common features of other buildings clustered within the inner bailey of a large castle. One of these was the chapel, where the lord and his family attended mass each morning. At first, small rooms within the great hall itself served as chapels; however, many castles eventually erected larger versions, one of the most popular having the chapel extend outward from one end of the hall, the two structures forming an L. Other inner structures and features of a large castle often included a stable, barn, laundry, brewery, dovecote (pigeon house), mill, and slaughterhouse; workshops for smiths, wrights, joiners (furniture makers), and candle makers; servants' quarters and various storehouses; as well as gardens, orchards, and fishponds. As scholar Fiona MacDonald writes, "A great castle was rather like a small town. Inside its walls, you could find almost everything you needed."

5

MEDIEVAL WARFARE TRANSFORMED: CASTLES UNDER SIEGE AND IN RUIN

Large pitched battles involving thousands of soldiers, like that at Hastings in 1066, were relatively rare occurrences in medieval warfare. For the most part, when fighting did occur, it concentrated around castles, since these fortresses were the supply depots, regional strongholds, and hubs of offensive and defensive strategy of the military strongmen of the day. The Gieses point out:

This medieval illustration depicts men and women defending a castle during a siege.

> It was often the offensive capabilities of the castle that provoked sieges, but it was its incomparable defensive strength that conferred its military importance. Always ready, requiring little maintenance and repair, demanding scant advance notice of impending attack, the castle remained the basic center of power throughout the Middle Ages.

The offensive and defensive weapons, tactics, and strategies of castle sieges constitute some of the most characteristic, evocative, and fascinating aspects of medieval society. And the disappearance of these weapons and tactics, as such sieges, along with castles themselves, eventually declined in importance, is among the most conspicuous features of Europe's transformation from medieval to modern times.

ASSAULT BY "SAPPERS," "BEARS," AND "HEDGEHOGS"

As a siege began, the attackers naturally directed their best ef-
forts at exploiting the castle's structural weaknesses; although
there were usually very few such vulnerable points, a stubborn
and vigorous enough assault on them had at least a chance of
success. The most common built-in weakness of many castles
was their having been erected over soft subsoil. Unless a fortress
rested on a large outcropping of solid rock, as a few, including
mighty Chepstow Castle, did, some of its walls were vulnerable
to sapping, or undermining. The usual procedure was to dig a
long tunnel, aiming if possible at a tower or corner in a curtain
wall. According to John Burke:

> Driving a passage through dangerously unstable earth, the
> sappers used timbers to prop up the roof. . . . When they
> reached the target area the tunnel was packed with
> branches, brushwood, rags, grease—anything which would
> burn—and the whole mass set ablaze. The sappers retired
> as speedily as miners always do when a charge has been
> fired. If all went well, the timbers burned through and col-
> lapsed, and into the weakened earth collapsed also a wall
> tower or a corner of the keep itself. Once such a breach had
> been made, the assault forces were concentrated there.

This sounds fairly easy and straightforward. In reality, however,
sapping was a slow process; when King John besieged
Rochester Castle in 1215, for instance, the mine his men dug,
though ultimately successful, took over six weeks to complete.
Sapping was also uncertain and dangerous; sometimes the diggers' aim was off and they ended up in the wrong place; while
even more often their tunnels prematurely collapsed, burying
them alive. The remains of an abandoned sap, from a siege that
took place in the summer of 1174, can still be seen at Bungay
Castle in Suffolk (in eastern England).

   If a castle was poorly manned or if the besiegers greatly out-
numbered the defenders, scaling ladders might be used to gain
entry. However, a great many ladders and men were needed
and the attack had to be very well coordinated and intense. And
even when besiegers met these conditions, they had to expect
heavy casualties. The defenders used arrows, rocks, and boiling
liquids to knock the attackers off the ladders and forked sticks
to push the ladders away from the walls.

Whenever possible, the attackers were better off to build wooden assault towers, called "belfries," "bears," or other colorful names. These were often identical in many ways with some of the siege towers employed in ancient times. Almost always assembled from materials gathered from the general vicinity, such towers gave the besiegers the advantages of height (they stood at least as high as the castle's walls) and cover from enemy fire (the wooden sides proved effective shields). Also, a large tower could deliver an enormous amount of offensive fire; one such belfry used at the siege of Kenilworth Castle in 1266 held two hundred troops and eleven catapults and may have been almost as imposing as the renowned version used by the ancient Greek siege expert Demetrius.

Yet siege towers also had their disadvantages. Such towers were extremely heavy and difficult to move over rough ground

Assault towers, supported by archers (both inside and outside the towers) and primitive cannons, assail the battlements of a besieged castle.

or uphill, and because they were composed mainly of wood, the defenders could and often did set them ablaze. What is more, towers could not be wheeled over a moat. To eliminate this barrier, besiegers sometimes filled in the moat with debris; since while doing so they were open to a shower of missiles from the walls, they approached slowly in heavily protected wheeled shelters known as "cats," "rats," "tortoises," or "hedgehogs."

A LETHAL RAIN OF MISSILES

When a castle was particularly strong, besiegers often either abandoned the above methods or supplemented them with artillery—siege machines that hurled stones and other projectiles at or over the walls. Several types of sophisticated artillery engines developed in Europe in the eleventh and twelfth centuries (influenced by Eastern models, which themselves had been inherited from Greek and Roman times). All were constructed of wood, which meant that the besieging army had to bring along or find many skilled wrights. During one of his military campaigns, England's King Henry II assembled over five hundred wrights to build the artillery he needed to attack a rebel castle.

Among the most common artillery engines were the ballista, essentially a giant crossbow or spear-thrower, and the mangon (or mangonel), or catapult, which hurled large rocks. They operated on the principles of greatly increasing either the torsion (twisting) of ropes or the tension (stretching) of wooden levers; the burst of energy produced on suddenly releasing the ropes or levers sent the projectile on its deadly flight. A large mangon could hurl heavy rocks up to thirteen hundred feet. Even more devastating was the trebuchet, introduced into western Europe in the twelfth century and here described by Hugh Braun:

> This was a huge affair of great timber balks [beams] built up into a lofty trestle, at the summit of which was supported a long balanced beam. The shorter end of the beam was weighted with a large box of earth or stones. The longer end, which held the projectile, was hauled down in the same fashion as . . . the mangon; when released, the weight revolved the beam and flung the projectile. Its velocity was generally increased by the attachment of a long leather sling to the end of the beam.

Large catapults are here shown in use during the storming of a crusader fortress. Note the men in the foreground turning a winch to increase the tension on the device's throwing arm.

These trebuchets could throw a projectile weighing perhaps half a ton, and ranges of a quarter of a mile are recorded. The deadly feature of the trebuchet, however, was its high trajectory, which enabled it to hurl its projectiles over the top of any stockade.

The frightening and lethal rain of missiles from these large artillery pieces are described in some surviving medieval tracts. "At last the large machine was put up," wrote the thirteenth-

OPERATING THE TREBUCHET

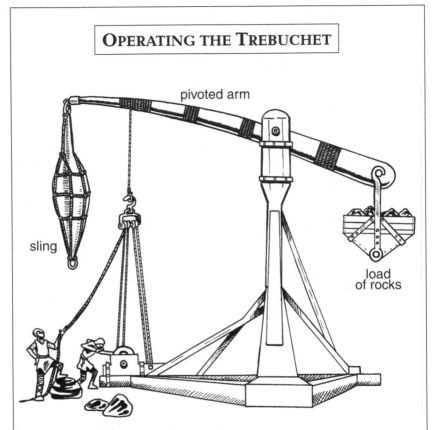

pivoted arm

sling

load
of rocks

The trebuchet operated by means of a counterweight (load of rocks) on the short
end of the beam (pivoted arm) and a sling holding the projectile on the long end.
When the rope holding the long end was released, the counterweight dropped,
swinging the beam forward and flinging the projectile.

century German chronicler Henry of Livonia, "and great rocks
were cast at the fort. The men in the fort, seeing the size of the
rocks, were seized with great terror." At another siege, at Fellin
in Estonia, said Henry, "the Germans built a machine, and, by
hurling stones night and day, they broke down the fortifications
and killed innumerable men and animals in the fort, since the
Estonians had never seen such things and had not strengthened
their houses against such attacks." Trebuchets also flung dis-
eased animals into castles in hopes of infecting the defenders.

Combining many different assault techniques and machines
and pressing the attack relentlessly and vigorously often
achieved the desired goal within a few weeks or months. The

following vivid account of the fall of Lord Falkes de Bréauté's castle at Bedford (about forty miles north of London) to the forces of King Henry III in 1224 after an eight-week siege is taken from the chronicle known as the *Annals of Dunstable*.

> On the eastern side was a stone-throwing machine and two mangonels which attacked the [new] tower every day. On the western side were two mangonels which reduced the old tower. A mangonel on the south and one on the north made two breaches in the walls nearest them. Besides these, there were two wooden machines

MEDIEVAL HEAVY ARTILLERY

Here, from his comprehensive *The Art of War in the Western World*, military historian Archer Jones describes the workings of the artillery commonly used in medieval sieges before the introduction of the trebuchet.

Until the beginning of the twelfth century, the only known kinds of artillery were catapults worked by torsion and tension. A torsion catapult used a heavy timber frame with a mass of twisted rope strung across near the front. In this twisted rope the builder secured one end of a movable beam having a spoon-shaped hollow on its other end. Operators pulled this free end backward and down by a large winch at the rear of the frame, against the resistance of the twisted ropes, and placed the stone to be thrown in the spoon-shaped cavity. They then released the free end of the movable beam by releasing a catch. The force of the twisted ropes then made the beam describe an upward and forward curve, moving fast enough to flip off the stone at a high angle of elevation. Such a catapult was known as a mangon, mangonel, or sling. Of course the projectiles were seldom uniform in weight, and weather affected the ropes. Accordingly, the shots of this type of machine dispersed so widely that it was generally used for bombarding large objectives, such as towns or castles. A tension catapult, usually known as a ballista, consisted of an exaggerated bow wound up by winches. It shot bolts or enormous arrows with great force, flat trajectory, and considerable accuracy. Although they could not penetrate walls, they were used by besiegers and besieged against small, fairly distant objectives, such as men out of range of infantry weapons.

erected . . . overlooking the top of the tower and the castle for the use of the crossbowmen and scouts. In addition there were very many engines there in which lay hidden both crossbowmen and slingers. Further, there was an engine called a cat, protected by which underground diggers . . . undermined the tower and castle. Now the castle was taken by four assaults. In the first the barbican was taken, where four or five of the outer guard were killed. In the second the outer bailey was taken, where more were killed, and in this place our people captured horses . . . crossbows, oxen, bacon, live pigs and other things beyond number. But the buildings with grain and hay in them they burned. In the third as-

Scaling ladders, hedgehogs, siege towers, and other weapons and devices are visible in this illustration of the siege of a fortified town from a fifteenth-century chronicle.

sault, thanks to the action of the miners, the wall fell near the old tower, where our men got through the rubble and amid great danger occupied the inner bailey. Thus employed, many of our men perished. . . . At the fourth assault . . . a fire was set under the tower by the miners so that smoke broke through into the room of the tower where the enemy were; and the tower split so that cracks appeared. Then the enemy, despairing of their safety . . . yielded [surrendered] to the king's command.

THE PLIGHT OF THE BESIEGED

The degree of success in withstanding a fully mounted siege like the one that overwhelmed Bedford Castle depended on the strength of the castle's walls, the size of its garrison, the amount of supplies it had stored, and the determination of the defenders. Even if the inhabitants managed to beat back many assaults, the possibility of ultimate defeat was still high. Once surrounded, a castle with many people and animals cramped inside and possessing too few supplies soon faced the prospects of starvation, malnutrition, and disease. Desperate defenders were known to resort to eating their horses and dogs, and eventually mice, rats, and grass. The attackers often managed to poison the castle's well; or the well dried up from overuse, the cause of the fall of Exeter Castle (170 miles southwest of London) in 1137 after a three-month-long siege. Moreover, under such crowded conditions, the latrines usually backed up, increasing the likelihood of sickness and producing a foul stench. Morale was another important factor. As Fiona MacDonald explains, during a siege

> the castle defenders lived in a state of constant uncertainty. They were cut off from contact with the outside world, and so did not know how well, or how badly, their allies were faring. The enemy forces camped outside the walls would do their best to depress them, by jeering, or by spreading false rumors.

Yet while such deprivations, coupled with the relentless pounding of the enemy's siege machines, brought about the fall of many castles, the fact is that some fortresses managed to survive these ordeals. Many of them had their own artillery pieces in place on the battlements. During Edward I's reign, for example, engineers added four catapults to Chepstow Castle's towers.

During sieges at various castles, such catapults, as well as ballistae and trebuchets, all of which had the added advantage of firing from a great height, often hurled back the very same rocks and spear bolts that the attackers had earlier lobbed into the strongholds. Castle defenders also regularly exploited the firepower of the crossbow, which had an effective range of between three and four hundred yards. Although besiegers used this weapon, too, it was much more effective in the hands of the besieged, who had the advantage of firing both from a height and from behind the protection of arrow loops.

Some castles avoided capture by exploiting a logistical reality of all warfare, namely the ratio of the amount of food available to the number of mouths to feed. When a castle was extremely well stocked with supplies, ironically the besiegers often faced starvation before the besieged. "Some castles kept a year's supply of food or even more on hand," the Gieses point out,

A highly stylized medieval illustration shows besiegers attacking a castle from both sea and land while the defenders fire at them from a crenellated tower.

and the relatively small size of a thirteenth-century garrison often meant that in a prolonged siege the assailants rather than the besieged were confronted with a supply problem. A garrison of sixty men could hold out against an attacking force ten times its number, and feeding sixty men from a well-stocked granary supplemented by cattle, pigs, and chickens brought in at the enemy's approach might be far easier than feeding 600 men from a war-ravaged countryside.

An example of a siege failing in the face of a combination of superior firepower, ample supplies, and sheer courage and determination occurred in 1216. Louis, dauphin of France, crossed the English Channel and laid siege to Dover Castle, on England's southern coast. Louis's forces encountered such massive and lethal defensive fire that they were forced to move their camp back from its original position; and in the face of the castle's continued strong and heroic resistance, the French finally gave up and lifted the siege.

THE DEMISE OF THE CASTLE

Eventually such sieges became outmoded, primarily because castles themselves became so. Many theories have been advanced to explain why the traditional medieval castle declined in importance and largely stopped being built at the end of the medieval era. One often-cited reason is the emergence of firearms, in particular the cannon, invented in Germany in the

CROSSBOWS VERSUS LONGBOWS

Sidney Toy, a widely recognized expert on castle lore, offers this comparison of the effectiveness of crossbows and longbows in siege warfare in his *Castles: Their Construction and History*.

Among the hand weapons in use during the Middle Ages the bow and arrow still held a strong position, and that long after the introduction of the crossbow. . . . The crossbow was in general use [in Europe] by the end of the twelfth century and, except among the English, was the favorite [hand] weapon from that time to the latter part of the fifteenth century. In open warfare the English preferred the longbow, which was about 6 ft. long. The longbow was light while the crossbow was heavy and cumbersome. With the longbow the archer could shoot about five arrows while the crossbow was discharging one bolt, and he could keep his eye on the foe during the adjustment of a new missile, while the crossbowman's whole attention was required for this purpose. In the defense of fortifications, however, where the crossbowman would have support for his bow and himself be secure from attack, the crossbow, with its heavier missile, greater force, and longer range was by far the superior weapon. The effective range of the longbow was about 220 yards, that of the fifteenth-century crossbow was from 370–380 yards, and with some bows even greater.

early 1300s. Early cannons were relatively feeble and inaccurate and had little effect on castle or town stone fortifications, as evidenced by the response by the chronicler of the German city of Ulm to a cannon attack in 1380: "A knight came and besieged the town and shot at it with thunder guns. It did no harm."

However, cannon technology rapidly advanced, and the lethal effects of cannon fire grew apace. In 1414 the cannon of a German prince demolished the castle of a rebellious vassal in just two days, an unprecedented event. And far larger and more destructive cannon attacks soon followed, both revolutionizing warfare and shocking military strategists and engineers across Europe. In the late 1440s, in the closing stages of the Hundred Years' War, French cannons reduced the English strongholds in northern France with amazing speed. Then came the even more astonishing fall of Christianity's great Eastern bastion, Constantinople, to the Ottoman Turks, led by Sultan Mehmed II, in 1453. The sultan, writes renowned Byzantine scholar John Julius Norwich, subjected the city's ancient, majestic, and supposedly impregnable walls to

> a bombardment unprecedented in the history of siege warfare. By the evening of the first day he had reduced to rubble a section near the Charisius Gate. . . . The bombardment [continued] uninterruptedly for the next forty-

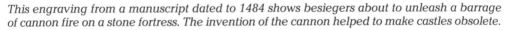

This engraving from a manuscript dated to 1484 shows besiegers about to unleash a barrage of cannon fire on a stone fortress. The invention of the cannon helped to make castles obsolete.

DRUMS, TRUMPETS, AND THE THUNDER OF ARTILLERY

Here, from the concluding section of his massive and magnificent *Decline and Fall of the Roman Empire*, the great English historian Edward Gibbon describes the Ottoman Turks' use of cannons against the Greek defenders in the last dramatic moments of Constantinople's fall on "the memorable twenty-ninth of May, in the fourteen hundred and fifty-third year of the Christian era." From this momentous event, Europe learned a hard lesson: If the mighty walls of this last bastion of the once mighty Roman Empire could not stand up to massed cannons, even the strongest castles were doomed.

> The troops, the cannon, and the fascines [bundles of twigs for filling in the moat] were advanced to the edge of the ditch [moat], which in many parts presented a smooth and level passage to the breach [made in the walls by earlier cannon fire]. . . . At daybreak, without the customary signal of the morning gun, the Turks assaulted the city by sea and land. . . . The ditch was filled with the bodies of the slain; they supported the footsteps of their companions. . . . The cries of fear and of pain were drowned in the martial music of drums [and] trumpets. . . . From the [infantry] lines, the galleys [warships], and the bridge, the Ottoman artillery thundered on all sides; and the camp and city, the Greeks and the Turks, were involved in a cloud of smoke, which could only be dispelled by the final deliverance or destruction of the Roman Empire. . . . The number of the Ottomans was fifty, perhaps a hundred, times superior to that of the Christians; the double walls were reduced by the cannon to a heap of ruins. . . . It was thus, after a siege of fifty-three days, that Constantinople . . . was irretrievably subdued by the arms of Mohammed [Mehmed] the Second.

eight days. Although some of the larger [cannon] pieces could be fired only once every two or three hours, the damage they did was enormous; within a week the outer wall across the Lycus had collapsed in several places, and although the defenders worked ceaselessly to repair the damage behind makeshift wooden stockades it was already clear that they could not do so indefinitely.

Still more advanced cannons were introduced with devastating effect in 1494, when France's Charles VIII invaded Italy and rapidly reduced castle after castle, some in as little as eight hours. By this time the handwriting was clearly on the wall for traditional castle builders. As Braun puts it, a castle's "lofty towers and curtains offered too large a target for the great guns, and the inherent lack of stability of tall structures made them a prey to the powerful blows of the new artillery."

Some historians have pointed out that the effects of advancing cannon technology were fairly gradual and that the advent of this weapon was not the only factor in the demise of medieval castles. Indeed, other military changes, as well as profound social and economic ones, swept through Europe in the fourteenth and fifteenth centuries: warfare became increasingly centered, as it had been in ancient times, around large pitched battles fought on open terrain; the manorial system began to break down, many former serfs becoming free farmers or merchants; and military leaders began to rely less on vassal knights and more on paid mercenary troops—all of these factors making large castles less important and/or too costly to maintain. Most important of all, perhaps, was the steady loss of the administrative and military power of local lords to central governments. One scholar suggests:

> The rapid growth of major political units around monarchies (or dictatorships) was based to a great extent on the rapid growth of European cities with their wealthy merchant classes, whose money taxes provided the wherewithal to hire and supply large mercenary armies equipped with expensive cannon. . . . The new political geography made obsolete many of the old frontier castles, such as those guarding the long-embattled English-Welsh and Norman-Breton-French borders.

ROMANCE SURVIVES

As the old medieval fortresses lost their importance, wealthy and powerful nobles built large, elegant, far-less-fortified palaces as residences. A few existing castles were transformed, at great expense, into imposing mansions; and some others became prisons. But most traditional castles were simply aban-

The towers and battlements of Italy's Castle of the Scaglieri create a picturesque, romantic vision of a vanished civilization.

doned. Of these, some, after falling into ruin, enjoyed a measure of restoration by governments anxious to preserve them as monuments of a glorious and romantic past. In England, for instance, as scholar Colin Platt tells us,

> it was in 1562 that Tickhill [a castle in Yorkshire, in northern England] was commanded to be maintained for no better reason than its worth as an "ancient monument." Early in the next century, when castles everywhere were being allowed to decay, the particular purpose of preserving Pontefract, another Yorkshire fortress, was "to prevent the ruin of a monument of such antiquity and goodly building."

Of the majority of castles that remained unused and were never refurbished, the ruins of most still dot European countrysides; for they were so massive and well built that even the ravages of six or more centuries have not been sufficient to erase them. Cracked, gray, and silent, yet splendid in their desolation, they stand as ghostly symbols of a bygone era of knights, lords, and sieges, an age whose harsher realities are often softened and romanticized by the hand of time. As John Burke so fittingly phrases it, "The horrors of . . . starvation during sieges and of death in foul dungeons, recede into the background when we contemplate the romantic silhouette of some old tower and battlements on the skyline. Romance survives; everyday reality conveniently fades."

GLOSSARY

arrow loop (or "murderess"): A narrow vertical slit in a castle wall through which defenders fired arrows and other missiles at attackers.

bailey: A courtyard, usually enclosed by a defensive wall.

ballista: A giant crossbow or spear-thrower.

barbican: An outwork or forward extension of a gate's walls, often forming an outer walled enclosure.

battlement (or parapet): The top of a defensive wall.

belfry (or bear): A wooden, wheeled assault tower used to deliver troops and offensive weapons to, and if possible over, a castle's walls.

bolster: A wide chisel used by stonemasons; they struck the bolster with a wooden mallet called a mell.

butler: The servant in charge of the buttery.

buttery: A chamber for storing and pouring wine and beer.

cat (also rat, tortoise, or hedgehog): A roofed, wheeled shelter used to protect attacking troops attempting to dig mines, fill in a moat, or operate a battering ram.

cistern: A reservoir for catching and storing rainwater.

crenellation: The notched effect in the battlements of castles and other medieval structures; the notches are called merlons, and the openings between them crenels.

curtain wall: An outer defensive wall enclosing a bailey or an entire castle or town.

dais: A raised platform, as in the lord's dais at one end of a great hall.

dead ground: The area directly outside a corner of a rectangular tower or curtain wall; attackers often approached through this zone because defenders on the walls at either side found it difficult to reach it with missiles.

drawbridge: A movable wooden platform spanning a moat in front of a castle's main gate; the most common version raised and lowered by means of chains worked by winches in a small chamber over the gate.

fealty: Loyalty.

garderobe (or privy): A latrine.

gong farmer: A latrine cleaner.

great hall (or hall): The principal living quarters of a medieval castle or house.

hewer: A mason who specialized in preparing stones for construction work; an ax man cut a stone, and a dresser shaped it.

hoarding (or hoard): A temporary wooden platform erected near or at the top of a battlement, usually resting on timbers projecting outward from holes in the wall.

homage: The ceremony in which a vassal swore loyalty to his lord.

keep (or donjon): The inner, usually highly fortified stronghold of a castle.

machicolation: An outward projection of masonry at the top of a defensive wall, the projection containing holes through which defenders dropped stones, fired missiles, and/or poured oil or other liquids.

mangon (or mangonel): A stone-throwing catapult.

manor: An estate held by a lord and farmed by his tenants.

manorial system: The arrangement whereby a lord allowed serfs and other workers to farm portions of his land, in return for which they gave him a share of their harvests and performed various duties and services.

master-mason: In medieval times, a combination of architect, building contractor, and general overseer.

motte: An earthen mound on which early castles were built; because most of these had an adjoining lower bailey, they became known as "motte-and-bailey" castles.

oppidum (plural oppida): Early northern European hill forts made of banks of earth reinforced with layers of timber and fieldstones.

pantry: A chamber for storing and slicing bread.

perch: A wooden peg on which to hang clothes.

plumber: A craftsman who fashioned lead pipes and sheeting.

portcullis: A heavy grated door, usually of oak shod with iron, raised and lowered vertically in a castle's main gateway.

sapper: A miner who dug tunnels (saps) beneath a castle's walls in hopes of causing them to collapse.

serf: An agricultural worker tied to a lord's land and bound to serve him for life.

setter: A mason who specialized in the actual assembly of walls and other stone structures.

shell keep: A small castle composed of a single circular wall enclosing an inner bailey, usually built atop a hill.

smith: A craftsman who fashioned and installed brackets and other items made of iron.

solar: At first, the private bedchamber of the lord and lady of a castle; later, any such chamber on an upper story.

squint: A peephole in a wall or floor.

steward (or seneschal): The general supervisor of a lord's estate and household.

stockade (or palisade): A fence enclosure composed of logs or wooden planks set vertically in the ground; for example, the enclosure protecting a motte-and-bailey castle.

tallow: Melted animal fat, often used to make candles.

toolings: Parallel grooves etched into stones by masons.

trebuchet: A large siege machine consisting of a wooden framework that supported a long balanced beam; the short end of the beam was weighted with a box of stones; the long end, holding a projectile, was pulled down and then released, sending the missile flying in a high arc.

trundle (or truckle): A portable bed, usually on wheels.

truss: A triangular wooden roof support.

vassal (or retainer): In the feudal system, a follower whom a lord granted the use of revenue-producing land (a fief or fee) in return for fealty (loyalty) and military service.

wright: A carpenter.

FOR FURTHER READING

Timothy Levi Biel, *The Age of Feudalism*. San Diego: Lucent Books, 1994.

Christopher Gravett, *Knight*. New York: Knopf, 1993.

Gertrude Hartman, *Medieval Days and Ways*. New York: Macmillan, 1960.

Gallimard Jeunesse et al., *Castles*. New York: Scholastic, 1990.

Fiona Macdonald and Mark Bergin, *A Medieval Castle*. New York: Peter Bedrick Books, 1990.

Don Nardo, *Life on a Medieval Pilgrimage*. San Diego: Lucent Books, 1996.

Jay Williams, *Life in the Middle Ages*. New York: Random House, 1966.

———, *The Siege*. New York: Little, Brown, 1954.

Jay Williams and Margaret B. Freeman, *Knights of the Crusades*. New York: American Heritage, 1962.

WORKS CONSULTED

Charles H. Ashdown, *European Arms and Armor*. New York: Barnes and Noble, 1995.

Kenneth J. Atchity, ed., *The Renaissance Reader*. New York: HarperCollins, 1996.

Robert Bartlett, *The Making of Europe: Conquest, Colonization, and Cultural Change, 950–1350*. Princeton, NJ: Princeton University Press, 1993.

John Betjeman, *A Pictorial History of English Architecture*. New York: Macmillan, 1972.

Morris Bishop, *The Middle Ages*. Boston: Houghton Mifflin, 1968.

Hugh Braun, *An Introduction to English Medieval Architecture*. New York: Frederick A. Praeger, 1968.

John Burke, *Life in the Castle in Medieval England*. New York: Dorset Press, 1992.

Julius Caesar, *Commentaries on the Gallic War*. Published as *War Commentaries of Caesar*. Translated by Rex Warner. New York: New American Library, 1960.

Norman F. Cantor, *The Medieval Reader*. New York: Harper-Collins, 1994.

Andreas Cappelanus, *The Art of Courtly Love*. Translated by J. J. Parry. New York: Columbia University Press, 1941.

G. G. Coulton, *Medieval Village, Manor, and Monastery*. New York: Harper and Row, 1960.

L. Sprague de Camp, *The Ancient Engineers*. New York: Ballantine Books, 1963.

Hans Delbrück, *Medieval Warfare*. Translated by Walter J. Renfroe Jr. Lincoln: University of Nebraska Press, 1982.

George Duby, ed., *Revelations of the Medieval World*. A History of Private Life, vol. 2. Translated by Arthur Goldhammer. Cambridge, MA: Harvard University Press, 1988.

Robin Fedden and John Thomson, *Crusader Castles*. London: John Murray, 1957.

Anne Fremantle, *Age of Faith*. New York: Time, 1965.

Sir John Froissart, *The Chronicles of England, France, and Spain*. H. P. Dunster's condensation of the Thomas Johnes's translation. New York: E. P. Dutton, 1961.

Edward Gibbon, *The Decline and Fall of the Roman Empire*. Great Books of the Western World, vols. 40 and 41. Chicago: Encyclopaedia Britannica, 1952.

Joseph Gies and Frances Gies, *Life in a Medieval Castle*. New York: Harper and Row, 1974.

———, *Life in a Medieval City*. New York: Harper and Row, 1969.

V. H. H. Green, *Medieval Civilization in Western Europe*. New York: St. Martin's Press, 1971.

Sir John Hackett, ed., *Warfare in the Ancient World*. New York: Facts On File, 1989.

Elizabeth Hallam, ed., *The Plantagenet Chronicles*. New York: Weidenfeld and Nicolson, 1986.

Friedrich Heer, *The Medieval World: Europe 1100–1350*. Translated by Janet Sondheimer. New York: New American Library, 1961.

Herodotus, *The Histories*. Translated by Aubrey de Sélincourt. New York: Penguin Books, 1972.

Donald Hill, *A History of Engineering in Classical and Medieval Times*. London: Routledge, 1996.

George Holmes, ed., *The Oxford History of Medieval Europe*. New York: Oxford University Press, 1989.

Archer Jones, *The Art of War in the Western World*. New York: Oxford University Press, 1987.

Charles W. Jones, *Medieval Literature in Translation*. New York: Longmans, Green, 1950.

John Keegan, *A History of Warfare*. New York: Random House, 1993.

Peter Kidson and Peter Murray, *A History of English Architecture*. New York: Arco Publishing, 1963.

William MacDonald, *The Architecture of the Roman Empire*. New Haven, CT: Yale University Press, 1982.

Edward T. McLaughlin, *Studies in Medieval Life and Literature.* Freeport, NY: Books for the Libraries Press, 1972.

David Nicholas, *The Medieval West, 400–1450: A Preindustrial Civilization.* Homewood, IL: Dorsey Press, 1973.

Nikolaus Pevsner, *An Outline of European Architecture.* Baltimore: Penguin Books, 1966.

Colin Platt, *Atlas of the Medieval World.* New York: St. Martin's Press, 1979.

———, *The Castles of Medieval England and Wales.* New York: Barnes and Noble, 1996.

Plutarch, *Lives*, excerpted in *Plutarch: Makers of Rome.* Translated by Ian Scott-Kilvert. New York: Penguin Books, 1965.

Polybius, *The Histories*, excerpted in *The Rise of the Roman Empire.* Translated by Ian Scott-Kilvert. New York: Penguin Books, 1979.

James B. Ross and Mary M. McLaughlin, eds., *The Portable Medieval Reader.* New York: Viking Press, 1972.

Marjorie Rowling, *Life in Medieval Times.* New York: Berkley Publishing, 1968.

Howard Saalman, *Medieval Architecture.* New York: George Braziller, 1965.

Gerald Simons, *Barbarian Europe.* New York: Time, 1968.

R. C. Smail, *Crusading Warfare, 1097–1193.* New York: Cambridge University Press, 1977.

R. W. Southern, *The Making of the Middle Ages.* New Haven, CT: Yale University Press, 1973.

Hans Straub, *A History of Civil Engineering.* London: L. Hill, 1952.

Brian Tierney, ed., *The Middle Ages.* Vol. 1, *Sources of Medieval History.* New York: Knopf, 1970.

———, *The Middle Ages.* Vol. 2, *Readings in Medieval History.* New York: Knopf, 1970.

Sidney Toy, *Castles: Their Construction and History.* New York: Dover, 1984.

Vitruvius, *On Architecture*. 2 vols. Translated by Frank Granger. Cambridge, MA: Harvard University Press, 1962.

Philip Warner, *The Medieval Castle: Life in a Fortress in Peace and War*. London: Barker, 1971.

John Warry, *Warfare in the Classical World*. Norman: University of Oklahoma Press, 1995.

Eugen Weber, ed., *The Western Tradition: From the Ancient World to Louis XIV*. Boston: D. C. Heath, 1965.

Lynn White Jr., *Medieval Technology and Social Change*. London: Oxford University Press, 1962.

Clara Winston and Richard Winston, *Daily Life in the Middle Ages*. New York: American Heritage, 1975.

INDEX

ease of building, 47
first Norman castles in England and, 30
limited living areas in, 28, 37

Norman Conquest, 28–29, 30, 32, 40, 47
building of castles and, 41
see also Battle of Hastings
Normandy, 27
Norwich, John Julius, 80

Palestine, 16, 38, 42, 43
Pembroke Castle, 49
Philip II (king of France), 9, 65, 66
Platt, Colin, 83
Plutarch, 20
Polybius, 19–20
portcullis, 20–21, 43–44, 52, 55

Restormel Castle, 31, 33
Revelations of the Medieval World (Barthélemy), 67
Richard I (king of England), 9, 64
Rochester Castle, 17, 70
Romans, 19, 20
decline of empire and, 23, 26, 81
knowledge of, utilized by Byzantines, 24
practicality of, 21–22
Rowling, Marjorie, 38

sanitation, 28
bathing, 63–64
latrine drains, 64–66
Saumur Castle, 66
scaffolding, 32
Scott, W. B., 32
sheerlegs hoist, 21, 22, 55
shell keeps. *See under* keeps
sieges, 14, 37, 69–70, 76, 83
advances in methods of, 17–18
artillery engines and, 72–77
catapults and, 18, 72, 75, 78
defense against, 28, 43–44, 77–79
food supplies and, 78

role of firearms in demise of, 79, 82
sapping and, 70
use of belfries and, 71–72
see also cannons; curtain walls; towers; trebuchet
Sirmione Castle, 83
Syracuse, 8, 19, 20, 44
Syria, 8, 52

Templars, 43
Tickhill Castle, 9, 83
Tierney, Brian, 35
Tigris–Euphrates river valley, 13
towers, 16, 24
crenellated, 44, 78
projecting, 45
siege, 17–18, 42, 71–72
see also portcullis; White Tower
Toy, Sidney, 14, 25, 32–33
trebuchet, 72–73, 74, 78
Troy, 14, 49–50
Trojan Horse and, 15, 16
Turkey, 12

Urban II (pope), 42

Vitruvius, Marcus Pollio, 22–23, 54–55

Wales, 46, 47, 49, 50
Warry, John, 18–19, 24–25
Watkins, Trevor, 12–13
Weber, Eugen, 37
Western Tradition, The (Weber), 37
White Tower (London), 49, 62, 64
William the Conqueror, 30, 40, 41, 43
campaign of castle building and, 29
as victor in Battle of Hastings, 8, 28
Winchester Castle, 62
windows, 66, 67, 68
Winston, Clara and Richard, 34–35
wooden hill forts, 27, 28, 29, 33

PICTURE CREDITS

ABOUT THE AUTHOR

Historian and award-winning writer Don Nardo has published many books about the ancient and medieval worlds, including *Life in Ancient Rome*, *Greek and Roman Mythology*, *The Battle of Marathon*, *Life on a Medieval Pilgrimage*, and *The Trial of Joan of Arc*, as well as one other volume in the Lucent Building History series, *The Roman Colosseum*. Mr. Nardo also writes screenplays and composes music. He lives with his wife, Christine, and dog, Bud, on Cape Cod, Massachusetts.